Spas That Heal

By the same author

HERBS THAT HEAL

SPAS THAT HEAL

William A. R. Thomson, M.D.

ADAM AND CHARLES BLACK
LONDON

First published 1978
A & C Black Limited
35 Bedford Row, London WC1R 4JH

ISBN 0 7136 1810 8

Thompson, William Archibald Robson
Spas that heal.
1. Health resorts, watering-places, etc. – Great Britain – History
I. Title
613.1'2 RA848

ISBN 0-7136-1810-8

Printed in Great Britain by
Hazell & Watson & Viney Ltd, Aylesbury, Bucks

Contents

List of illustrations

Preface

Since mankind's earliest days he has appreciated and made use of the soothing, healing properties of water, whether as a means of applying heat or cold for the relief of pain, for its pain-relieving massaging effect, or to cleanse his wounds. He also early realized that waters differed in their healing properties according to their varying content. This belief in the healing qualities of water he took over from the animal world and incorporated in his religious beliefs.

All the great civilizations of the world have made use of the healing powers of water, and today in Europe spas play an important role in medical treatment. Indeed, they are flourishing as they have never done before. Their clientele may be changing. The kings, queens, princesses and grandees of the past may have been replaced by commoners of all social classes, but governments on both sides of the Iron Curtain, as well as their medical advisers, still consider that they are a sound health investment. This alone is an impressive argument in their favour. One finds it difficult to believe that, for example, the Austrian, French and German Governments would spend the large sums they do in defraying the cost of treating their nationals at spas if they were not convinced that they were getting value for money.

In Britain, however, the converse is true. Since the introduction of the National Health Service in 1948 British spas have been dying a lingering death. For this retrograde step the responsibility falls fairly and squarely on the shoulders of British rheumatologists. It is on their advice that successive Ministers of Health have closed down our spas.

The thesis, or contention, of this book is that they are wrong and unjustified in their repressive attitude. On the other hand, to be fair to them, it has been done with the best of intentions, forgetting, however, the old adage about the road to the nether regions being paved with such intentions. British spas have been spurned by the modern generation of rheumatologists on the grounds that they are unscientific – and this, in their eyes, is an unpardonable sin. What they ignore, or forget, is the cumulative evidence of literally millions of patients over the years who have benefited from treatment at spas.

Granted that spas have been abused, but what form of treatment has not been abused in its time by a certain proportion of the medical profession? Equally valid is the criticism that spa doctors have not been as conscientious as they might have been in producing evidence to support their claims. On the other hand, those scientific rheumatologists of today who are condemning spa therapy are doing so on equally invalid grounds. They have not produced a shred of convincing 'scientific' evidence to show that spa therapy is not as effective as the modern methods they vaunt so proudly. Until they do so, they have no right to damn an old-established form of therapy such as that practised in spas. Apart from anything else, if British rheumatologists are right, then the vast majority of European doctors are wrong: an interesting commentary in these days of increasing integration of the medical professions of the E.E.C.

If these scientifically minded rheumatologists had produced any alternative to spa therapy the position might have been different, but what do we find? According to editorial comment in the *British Medical Journal*, 'There is no treatment for severe rheumatoid arthritis that is both safe and really effective . . . Against this background the pharmaceutical industry has sought to produce new drugs without the toxicity of aspirin . . . Numerous preparations have appeared for which these claims are made, usually heralded by sales promotion on a scale that leaves no doubt about the profits to be made from a product that enjoys even temporary popularity . . . In conclusion it is sadly necessary to point out how seldom the individual patient benefits from drug treatment to the extent implied in many drug advertisements – or indeed in many of the enthusiastic drug trial reports. And all these drugs are potentially toxic.' It might have added that spa therapy does not kill, nor does it have any side-effects – that euphonious euphemism that slips so glibly off the tongue of the modern layman.

Of course, there is a psychological factor in spa therapy (one of the criticisms of it by its opponents), but so there is in any form of treatment of a chronic condition such as rheumatism. But the psychological factor is only part of spa therapy. Further, to contend, as modern rheumatologists do, that there is no difference between the effects of ordinary water and the mineral waters of spas, and deny all the claims of patients to the contrary is, as already indicated, not justified.

Take, for example, the case of Mrs Ida Prins-Buttle, who led such a gallant rearguard action opposing the closing of the Bath Spa Treatment Centre in December 1976. An arthritic subject herself, she had been attending the Treatment Centre once a week since 1969. To those doctors who kept on telling her that a hot bath would provide just as much relief, she replied: 'I've had thousands of baths at home, and they don't help me the way the spa water does.' And I have had the same story from a retired physiotherapist – a profession which is renowned for its shrewdness and its contempt for any form of 'quackery'. Patients may not always be right, but no section of the medical profession has any right to damn their claims out of court without any valid evidence.

It is against this background that I have written this book. Its thesis is quite simple. There is a case for spa therapy, and our

British spas should be reopened. At the moment only one, Leamington, is acting officially as a spa subsidized by the National Health Service. One other, that at Buxton, is for all practical purposes giving spa therapy, but in a National Health Service hospital, not in the original spa treatment centre, while a third, that at Woodhall Spa, is subsidized by the National Health Service but is not using the unique spa water. In addition there are five other viable spas in the country: those at Bath, Droitwich, Harrogate, Llandrindod Wells and Strathpeffer. In other words, there are eight viable spas, all of which I have visited during the preparation of this book.

In writing the book I have avoided technicalities as far as possible. This is not a textbook of spa therapy. It is the story of spas that heal all down the ages, with the emphasis on the position today. It attempts to give a balanced picture of the present state of affairs and to show why our spas must be reopened if we are to do justice to the many rheumatic citizens in our midst. Not that rheumatism is the only condition that benefits from spa therapy, but it is a major health problem that is costing the nation far too much. And not the least of the reasons for this is the deliberate misguided closure of our many spas.

Much water has flowed under the bridges since I first became interested in this fascinating problem. Theories have come and gone, therapeutic fashions – some dangerous – have waxed and waned, but we are really little the wiser than in those days when I was a student. Certainly we do not know the cause of most of the rheumatic diseases. Neither is there a cure. All that we can do is to provide relief and comfort. This we can do, and one of the most effective ways of proving this is by developing our spas, and it is in the hope that it may speed up their return to a healing role that this book has been written, dedicated to all those who could benefit from our spas that heal.

I

How it all began

Water is essential to life. Without it death rapidly ensues. We can exist for relatively long periods without food, as hunger strikers have demonstrated, but without water the body rapidly disintegrates until death brings a welcome end to the hell-like agonies of ravaging, unquenchable thirst. The pangs of hunger can be quite unpleasant enough but they are as nothing compared with the agonies of thirst.

It is therefore not surprising that from its earliest beginnings the human race has had a profound respect for water. In its migrations it has been largely guided by the availability of water, and nothing was more welcome to our primeval foraging forebears than the sight of a spring of water at sundown. Not only was water necessary for human life, our ancestors soon discovered, it was also necessary for the survival of their flocks and their crops.

From these elementary observations it was not a long step to the idea that water had a curative action, and again primitive man learned much from his observations of the animals around him. How the wounded animal sought the healing effect of certain springs, whilst the exhausted animal at the end of a long trek wallowed in the lake or river and came forth refreshed, with his muscular activity restored. Equally he observed how certain springs appeared to have a particular attraction for certain animals, and it did not require a particularly high stage of cerebration to realize that this probably meant that the water in the spring contained certain healing constituents, or at least certain constituents essential to health. An age-old observation, incidentally, which led to the establishment of more than one modern spa, such as Cheltenham, or – though this may be more legend than fact – Bath. If the Bath tale is legend, the story of the royal leprosy-stricken swineherd being cured of his leprosy by bathing in the hot morass from which he observed his pigs emerging cured of their skin disease, is obviously an allegory based on this old tradition of the healing virtues of certain waters.

The next step was more or less inevitable: the attribution of supernatural and magical powers to water. Man has never lived by bread alone, and he has always required some supernatural power to fall back on to reassure him in the darkness of the night, the darkness of the spirit and the darkness of impending death. Water with its healing virtues, and its essentiality (to use a most expressive term that, regrettably, has dropped out of current usage) was the natural gift of the gods, and the springs from which it gushed became the seats of gods, spirits or nymphs.

Thus began the great tradition of the spas that heal and, as one American commentator has noted, 'There are few therapeutic agents that have been used continuously for thousands of years in virtually the same form and whose popularity has increased. Water is one of these agents if not the major one. There are more spas now than ever before, and more people visit them.' According to Abraham Lincoln, 'You can fool all the people some of the time, and some of the people all the time, but you cannot fool all the people all of the time.' There would not seem to be much stretching of the future President's aphorism (incidentally also attributed to Barnum, the king of showmen) to suggest that there must be something of value in a form of treatment which has retained its popularity all down the ages.

Before reviewing some of the more salient features in the origin and history of spas, a definition of the term is indicated. The

Oxford English Dictionary gives a triple definition: 'With capital. The name of a watering-place in the province of Liège, Belgium, celebrated for the curative properties of its mineral springs. 2. A medicinal or mineral spring or well. 3. A town locality, or resort possessing a mineral spring or springs.' Two contrasting definitions – one British and concise, the other North American and verbose – may be given from medical writings. The attractively concise British one is, 'A health resort with natural mineral waters of proved therapeutic value.' The North American equivalent is, 'A place where mineral-containing water flows from the ground naturally or to which it is pumped or conducted, and is then used for therapeutic purposes.' 'The word "spa"', it is added, 'may also be applied to a place where the therapeutic agent is mud or the water in a lake or sea.' Further, 'According to some,' it is stated, 'a spa is foremost a resort where the primary interest is health, where the waters may be artificial, or where climate, not water, is the principal treatment.' For the purposes of this book this last concept will be ignored.

The story behind the *Oxford English Dictionary*'s first definition is that in 1326 a Liège iron-master, named Collin Le Loupe, founded a health resort at the near-by fountain of chalybeate (or iron-containing) waters which he claimed had cured him. *Espa* is the old Walloon word for fountain, and in due course the town that arose around this fountain came to be known as Spa. Some two hundred years later a similar chalybeate well was discovered at Harrogate, and this was described as a spaw. A century or so later, Sheridan introduced the term for a mineral-water resort, and so it has been used ever since in the English-speaking world – but not in Continental Europe, where the usual description is the equivalent of thermal station. Various terms may be added to indicate a spa, such as *Bad* in Germany, *-les-Bains* in France, and *Terme* in Italy.

And now back to our historical review of the origin and development of spas that heal. There is no more convincing starting point than the fact that the Babylonian word for physician signified 'one who knows water'. In Greek mythology miraculous powers of healing were attributed to many springs, and there is a host of classical allusions to the value of water. Thus Homer records that Ulysses, on finding on his return from Ithaca that his father, Laertes, was in a poor state of health, immediately recommended warm bathing to restore him. By the fifth century B.C. this belief in healing waters was well incorporated in medical practice at the Asklepieia, as they were known, where patients came for treatment, practically all of which, including the famous one at Epidauros, contained baths and springs, and many of which were built near mineral or thermal springs.

The Romans took over the concept of the healing power of water in its entirety, preceded by the Etruscans who laid great stress on its therapeutic value. Baths soon became an established feature of Roman life and were developed on a massive scale. Thus the baths of Diocletian (A.D. 245–313) contained 3000 rooms. The procedure in these has been graphically and concisely described by Professor Ralph Major in *A History of Medicine*: 'The patrons in these baths first entered the *Apodyterium*, where they were undressed and massaged; then sent to the *Tepidarium*, which was warm and balmy; then to the warm *Sudatorium*, which produced marked sweating; then into the hot bath, the *Calidarium*; and finally into the cold bath, the *Frigidarium*.' By the time of the Emperor Constantine, towards the end of the Roman Empire, there were 860 baths and 11 large thermae in Rome.

While many of these were for hygienic purposes, leading Roman physicians, such as Galen, used spa therapy, the main indications for its use being disease of the joints and the urinary tract. There were also many spas scattered throughout Italy, such as Ischia and Baiae, and others farther afield. Pliny (A.D. 23–79), one of the great encyclopaedists of the Roman Empire (whose innate curiosity incidentally led to his death in the great Vesuvian eruption that destroyed Pompeii, as he insisted on going to see what was happening) records the hot springs at Wiesbaden and hot and cold springs in the Pyrenees.

The Baths of Diocletian, Rome, completed during the opening years of the fourth century A.D. The great central hall, the tepidarium, was 200 × 80 ft and 90 ft high. *Thermes de Diocletian* (Paris, 1877).

But perhaps Rome's greatest contribution to the propagation of spas were the baths which were built wherever her legions went. Around a hundred of them have been recorded, including Aquae Gratianae (Aix-les-Bains), Aquae Calidae (Vichy), Aquae Grani (Aachen), Aquae Augustae (Dax), Aquae Mattiacae (Wiesbaden), Aquae Pannonicae (Baden bei Wein), Aquae Sulis (Bath), Aurelia Aquensis (Baden-Baden), Aquineum (Budapest), and Vicus Aquarum (Baden in Switzerland). All of these survive to the present day among the leading spas of Europe.

Although these and other baths had their ups and downs during the Middle Ages, many of the public ones being closed during the epidemic of syphilis that swept over Europe in the latter part of the fifteenth century and the early part of the sixteenth century because they were aiding the spread of the disease, spa therapy never ceased. An indication of the esteem in which it was held is the fact that the first printed work on baths appeared as early as 1473, whilst another, by G. M. Savonarola, grandfather of the reformer, came out twelve years later.

Military leaders, including Charlemagne, made full use of baths for the treatment and rehabilitation of wounded soldiers, Henry IV of France founding a spa institute at Aix-les-Bains. This was a tradition that was long maintained, particularly in France and Germany, as is admirably exemplified in an interesting, little-known, medical footnote to the Crimean War.

This took the form of a 37-page pamphlet entitled *Military Sanatoria. Letter Addressed to H.R.H. the Duke of Cambridge, Commander-in-Chief, etc., on the Introduction of Mineral-Water Establishments for the Use of the Army*, by P. Pincoffs, M.D., M.R.C.P., etc., late Civil Physician to the Scutari Hospital, and published in 1856. In the course of this Dr Pincoffs draws attention to the fact that, 'In France and Germany, lengthened experience has shown that many soldiers whose constitutions are undermined by the wear and tear inseparable from military duty are often within a very short period restored to health by being sent to sanatoria established in thermal and other watering-places after having been treated for months to little or no purpose in excellent hospitals of the various stations.' In commending Dr Pincoffs' plea for 'military sanatoria', the *British and Foreign Medico-Chirurgical Review* quotes a French report as showing that 26 per cent of these patients were 'cured' while 48 per cent were 'relieved', adding: 'Thus 74 per cent of cases who had passed through the ordinary hospital treatment were decidedly benefited: cases which but for the sanatoria would probably have been allowed to linger out their lives as hopeless invalids.'

In the course of his 'letter' Dr Pincoffs produces a piece of statistical evidence that indicates that the so-called medical statistician of today is not such a novel innovation as he and his backers claim. To this French military practice he attributes the fact that France, with a standing army nearly three times as large as that of England, had 51,530 pensioners in 1856 compared with 59,987 in England. Even Florence Nightingale could not have put statistics to better use. In elaborating this point it is noted that, 'The larger proportion of our pensioners is chiefly owing to the system hitherto pursued of retaining a man in foreign service until his constitution is entirely broken, and then discharging and pensioning him; whereas he could have a fair chance of recovering his health and returning to duty were he sent home in time to such sanatoria as I propose.'

Dr Pincoffs' plan was the establishment of 'sanatoria' for invalided soldiers at thermal springs for the benefit of the wounded and diseased. In noting that France had such military sanatoria at six spas, the *British and Foreign Medico-Chirurgical Review* comments: 'It is especially to be remarked that the most favourable per-centage in the French figures already quoted is found among the rheumatic cases which nearly regards us as the most rheumatic nation in the world.' To which it adds its final commendation: 'It is, then, a very proper matter for consideration of our military authorities whether cause can be shown for the establishment of sanatoria for our own troops, either at home or abroad.'

Later the *Review* reported: 'We learn that a small experiment is already being carried out at Bath.' How far this 'small experiment' went is not recorded, but it certainly had no real practical results, and the War Office continued to show its traditional contempt of its medical advisers. Neither the concept nor Dr Pincoffs is mentioned in Sir Neil Cantlie's *History of the Army Medical Department*, though it is of interest that he records that practically 20 per cent of the 9544 soldiers invalided from the Crimean War were invalided on account of 'rheumatic disorders'.

That spas were not used indiscriminately is indicated by the fact that from around the seventeenth century a degree of specialization began to appear, some, for example, concentrating on the treatment of diseases of women, whilst sulphur waters were used for the treatment of chronic skin diseases such as eczema and psoriasis. Much later, in the nineteenth century, carbonic acid baths were introduced for the treatment of heart disease, first at Marienbad, and then becoming a much publicized specialty of Nauheim in Germany.

Over the centuries the popularity of spas has been enhanced by royal patronage, perhaps the most persistent in living memory being King Edward VII, though his mother was not averse to patronizing them both at home and abroad (Aix-les-Bains, for example). Some took more than a personal interest in them. Thus, Peter the Great was so impressed by the benefit he derived from treatment at Spa and Carlsbad that he ordered a search to be instituted for medicinal springs in Russia, while Maria Theresa, on the recommendation of her physician, had a list made of all the spas in Austria and their waters analysed.

In ancient times mineral springs were used for both drinking and bathing. Whilst the latter tended to predominate, there is evidence of drinking cures dating back several thousand years. Thus, excavations at St Moritz indicate that the water of an iron mineral spring was being drunk there some three thousand years ago, and the much-admired Buveur de Vichy in the Louvre is evidence of the habit being indulged in at Vichy at an early stage in its valetudinarian history. The famous Hippocratic school of medicine devoted considerable attention to the quality of water for drinking, classifying waters into alum, bituminous, effervescent, salt, and sulphur waters. In the later Greek and the Roman era they were drunk on a fairly large scale for conditions such as liver disease and stones in the kidneys and bladder.

During the Middle Ages bathing predominated in European spas until around the sixteenth century. Then, largely on account of the iatrochemical school of thought that then began to penetrate medical practice, drinking cures gradually came into vogue. Carlsbad was one of the first European spas to embark on this new development, when claims were made, around 1520, for the value of its waters in the treatment of diseases of the liver. The practice soon caught on, particularly for the treatment of dyspepsia and liver disease, with stone in the kidney and bladder as a side-line until, in the words of one commentator, 'Through the use of spas for gastroenterological symptoms, spas became more famous than they had been for baths. Even in a number of smaller spas, picturesque pavilions arose over springs; these were promenades with roofs, designed for drinking mineral waters during walks, and for social entertainments. The fame of Vichy and other spas grew, while that of the formerly great thermae, Baden-Baden in Germany and Baden in Switzerland, temporarily receded.'

Inevitably the method was abused and, presumably acting on the traditional principle still observed in certain developing countries, it was assumed that, if a little did you good, a lot would do you much more good. Hence heroic doses – up to a gallon – were consumed. As the waters were often quite strongly purgative, the results were often cataclysmic – if not catastrophic. In an age when orthodox medicine, or allopathy as it was known to differentiate it from homoeopathy, subjected its unfortunate victims to purging, bleeding and vomiting, these jumbo doses and their consequences were not looked upon as askance as they would be today.

In due course a modicum of moderation was introduced, more

attention was devoted to the constituents of mineral waters, and an attempt was made to correlate the constituents with their effects and adjust the dosage accordingly. Thus, alkaline waters were recommended for dyspepsia and liver and gall-bladder disease, as well as Glauber's salt and Epsom salt with their stronger purgative action. Simple effervescent waters and earthy mineral waters were recommended for stones in the kidneys and bladder, and iron, or chalybeate, waters were an obvious choice for the treatment of anaemia – particularly chlorosis, or green anaemia, the all too prevalent form of anaemia which afflicted so many young women in the Victorian era. In this context it must be remembered that until well into the nineteenth century doctors had relatively little choice in the matter of drugs, and the drinking of mineral waters naturally assumed a greater importance in the seventeenth and eighteenth centuries than it did subsequently, though the tradition still persisted at certain spas, such as Vichy, Carlsbad and Marienbad.

No account of 'drinking cures' would be complete without a passing reference to the bottling of mineral spring waters. This custom dates back at least to Roman days, when such waters were bottled and transported quite considerable distances. This was an inevitable development as the reputation of different waters spread abroad. People who could not go to spas demanded the benefit of the waters, and commercial exploiters were not slow to take advantage of, and stimulate, this demand. Some spas, such as Carlsbad, held out against the practice on the grounds that it would reduce its popularity with, and therefore its income from, visitors, but the majority were not averse to it.

For long, difficulties in bottling technique slowed up supplies, but these have been overcome and today bottled mineral waters are big business, and in Britain alone are estimated to be worth £3 million. Most of those available in the United Kingdom come from France where their production is rigidly controlled. These include Contrex, Evian, Perrier, Vichy and Vittel. The solitary British one bottled on anything like a large scale is Malvern, though Trefriw Wells in Wales is currently offering its water at £7 for a seven weeks' course, the cost being justified by the claim that it is 'particularly rich in iron and sulphur and so strong that you will only need to take about two tablespoonfuls per day'.

In the United States of America the concept of spas has never caught on in a big way. According to one United States physician, 'In general, there is considerable resistance upon the part of most American physicians to send their patients to spas for treatment.' According to another, this aversion is shared by patients, and is attributed to 'exaggerated commercialism and the general lack of competent medical advisers resident at spas'. In a way this is not surprising in a nation that lacks tradition and has an ingenuous faith in Science (with a capital 'S'). As one of the commentators just quoted put it, writing in the early 1960s: 'In this century, hydrotherapy has migrated from the spa and "Hydropathic Establishment" to the hospital, along with most other refined, professional therapeutic procedures. Divested of social exuberances, commercial enthusiasm, and medical duplicity, hydrotherapy in the United States is now largely integrated with hospital therapies, and, particularly in university and other research hospitals, an orderly, rational advance can be expected.' Whether this 'rational advance' has been achieved is another matter.

On a more homely note, and on the obverse side of the chromium-plated scientific coin, is the story of the most famous of all poliomyelitis victims: President Franklin D. Roosevelt. It begins with the visit to Warm Springs, Georgia, of a young victim of the disease. While there he accidentally fell from his wheelchair into the pool. In his desperate struggle to save himself from drowning he suddenly realized that he was moving his previously completely paralysed limbs. Thus 'motivated' he started taking exercises in the hot pool, and within a year he was up and about – ambulant, in technical jargon – on crutches and braces.

When the future President was stricken by poliomyelitis he was recommended to see whether the waters of Warm Springs would have a similar beneficial effect on him. He went, he consistently underwent his underwater exercises in the warm water and was so impressed by the results that he wrote an article entitled *Swimming Back to Health*. Needless to say, this put Warm Springs, Georgia, on the map, and the crippled of all classes of society flocked to it seeking cure, or at least alleviation, of their palsy.

To ensure that lack of funds should be no handicap to his fellow cripples, Mr Roosevelt established the Georgian Warm Springs Foundation in 1927, putting money into it himself, persuading many of his friends to do so also, and becoming president of the board of trustees. A story which is both a classical example of a spa that heals and of how the United States of America attempts to maintain an egalitarian state in a country devoted to private enterprise.

2

Religious wells

From earliest pagan days, wells and springs have been endowed with magical and sacred properties. In Britain they played a large part in the religious rites of the Druids and the Picts. The origin of this belief in their special properties is probably a combination of wonder and mystery at the sight of water welling out of the ground and a realization of how essential water is to life. This latter realization inevitably became linked with a belief in the healing and soothing property of water, as has already been discussed in chapter 1.

Inevitably the twentieth-century cynic, with that superficial knowledge of psychology that he is so fond of disporting, or rather flaunting, in public, has suggested – or rather declaimed, for modesty and reticence are anything but the hallmark of the species – that this respect for wells is phallic in origin. The ingenuous, perverse, or perverted reasoning advanced is that the well represents the female organ while the accompanying tree or pillar (by no means always present in fact, though presumably always to the fore in the cynic's sub-umbilical and/or subliminal mind) is the male organ. This harmless example of psychological juvenilia fails to comply with any of the reasonable standards of evidence that can legitimately be advanced, and can quickly be dismissed. The basis for it is probably a fact overlooked by its progenitors. This is that, by a natural association of ideas, running water suggests the passing of urine. This is an association that is often taken advantage of by doctors when they have a patient who has difficulty in passing urine, a sample of which is required for testing. Turning on the tap in a wash-basin in the room in which the patient is attempting to pass water almost inevitably produces the requisite specimen. In view of the identity of the external genitalia with both the passing of water and sexual intercourse, it is easy to see how the amateur psychologists have been misled.

What matters, and what is certain, is that to the pagan mind these wells were the abodes of gods and spirits, and it was this belief that the early Christian Fathers cashed in on by converting these sacred springs or wells to the purposes of the Christian faith. Thus St Columba, after washing his hands and feet in it, blessed one such well that had previously been a place of resort by pagan Picts who had dreaded and worshipped a malignant spirit that was supposed to dwell in its depths. In due course, after Columba's time, it became a popular pilgrimage site.

St Columba's example was widely followed by other Christian missionaries to the Picts. A common practice among them was for the missionary to establish his solitary cell beside a sacred spring, and in time these springs, scattered throughout Scotland, became identified with the names of special saints. Whether or not they contained medicinal substances, or were merely ordinary water, mattered not. From the earliest times the sick betook themselves to these springs or wells to which a saintly name was attached, for the purpose of being healed. Not infrequently the water was also used by the missionary to baptize converts, thus, as it has been said, 'capitalizing upon ancient superstition to serve the ends of the Church'. Equally it established from the early days of the Christian Church its traditional teaching of the 'cure' of souls and of bodies.

The extent to which this association between healing wells and the Christian Church developed and persisted is exemplified by the fact that in *Scotland in Early Christian Times*, Anderson's list of 'the principal holy wells' totted up to thirty. As Dr J. D.. Comrie, the well-known historian of Scottish medicine, comments: 'Most parishes in early days in Scotland were possessed of one or more of these holy pools or wells, to which resort was more or less commonly made for their healing virtues down to quite modern times.' 'A more striking instance', he adds, 'could hardly be given of the persistence of an ancient belief through all the changes in the form of religion and all phases of advancing intelligence and rationalism.' Equally valid would it be to point out that they provided a cheaper, more accessible, less painful and safer form of therapy than was available elsewhere. In contrast to the ignorant crudities of medieval medicine and the brutal aggressiveness of the eighteenth and early nineteenth centuries, these holy wells did at least give Nature a chance to exert her soothing propensities.

A glance at the record of some of these wells throws a fascinating light on how deeply ingrained in the human mind is this belief in the healing, if not necessarily curative, value of holy water. Thus, there is the well, or spring, of St Fillan, known as the 'leper' to distinguish him from St Fillan of Glendochart. St Fillan was a teacher of the sixth century of peculiar sanctity, specially celebrated in the care of disease. His spring at the foot of Dunfillan Hill, near Comrie, according to Dr Comrie, 'was much frequented even up to the eighteenth century, while to repose on his seat on the hill was regarded as a cure for rheumatism'. Another, 'till lately resorted to as a place of pilgrimage', according to Dr Comrie, was St Wallach's Well in the parish of Glass in Aberdeenshire, while St Maelrubha's Well on Innis Marce was famed for the cure of insanity. Holy Island, just offshore from Lamlash on the Isle of Arran in the Firth of Clyde, is so called because the hermit, Melio, lived in a cave on it, beside which was a holy well, for many centuries 'reckoned efficacious in the cure of disease'.

In view of the respect of the Celt for tradition – the cynic might prefer the term, superstition – it is not surprising that, certainly up to the seventeenth century, recourse to healing wells was a widespread habit among Highlanders. One of the most popular of these healing wells was at Loch Siant in Skye. Here people flocked from far and near seeking a cure for headaches, stones in the kidneys and bladder, and consumption, as well as many other ailments. Although some wells had a reputation for their efficacy in specific diseases, generality was the rule. Part of the cure at the Loch Siant well was to walk round it 'dessil', that is, following the direction of the sun, and only then to drink the water.

This circumambulation, of course, was an old pagan custom, which persisted well into the Christian era. Thus it was also one of the prescribed rituals at another famous well of this era on Islay, which had a reputation for the cure of all diseases. Here, however, the circumambulation occurred after the drinking. Such was its reputation that, even if the patient was unable to visit the well personally, its water was considered effective if a proxy was sent who, after performing all the appropriate actions, carried some of the water to be drunk by the sick person at home. Not the least interesting of the tales of this particular well is that it existed originally on Colonsay until, according to the chronicler of old, 'An impudent woman happened to wash her hands in it and, then immediately after, the well being thus abused, came in an instant to Islay.' The debunking of legend is a somewhat cruel custom, but is it possible that what happened was that the well on Colonsay dried up naturally, as many a well-known spa well has (for instance, that at Epsom and the one in Wanstead Park in Essex) and it was in a search for a substitute that the one on Islay was discovered?

It is Edinburgh, however, that can boast of perhaps the two most famous healing wells in Scotland. The tale of one of these, St Triduana's at Restalrig, is best told in the words of Dr Comrie, to whose *History of Scottish Medicine* I am indebted for much of the information in this chapter. 'St Triduana was a recluse of the primitive Church, whose tomb after her death became a shrine for pilgrims affected with eye diseases. In early life her beauty attracted a Pictish chief from whom she fled, and, being pursued by his emissaries, she plucked out her eyes and sent them to him impaled upon a thorn, as they had been the cause of his unwelcome attentions. For many centuries the well at Restalrig, afterwards called St Margaret's Well, was the resort of those who, in the words of Sir David Lindsay, went to "St Triad well to mend their ene".'

'So hard does tradition die,' Dr Comrie notes, 'that even now [1927] people with eye disorders frequently come with bottles to collect the water despite the fact that the ancient wellhouse has been removed to another spring [*circa* 1860] (St David's or the Rood Well) about a mile distant, close to Holyrood.' In passing, it is of interest to note that until quite recently yet another Edinburgh religious well was being patronized. This was St Bernard's Well in Stockbridge. Writing in 1919 one authority commented: 'The water is rather disagreeably sulphurous, but its use is largely restricted to a few old valetudinarians who go there more or less frequently for a morning draught with varying benefit.' To which he adds: 'Possibly if it had been situated in a fine country district it might have led to a spa, but in the centre of a big city it has been overlooked.' Certainly today its surroundings are not particularly prepossessing.

The other Edinburgh healing well is the Balm Well of St Catherine's Chapel at Liberton, or leper-town as it was originally known, from the fact that it was the site of a hospital for the victims of this dreaded disease. A near-by well at the Priest's Hill, or Grace Mount as it is now known, was celebrated throughout the Middle Ages for the treatment of skin diseases, and was almost certainly used by the leprosy patients in a vain attempt to rid themselves of their then incurable disease. Robert the Bruce, who probably had the disease, is said to have benefited from the use of the water. This claim to fame for the alleviation of skin diseases, if not leprosy, is not so far fetched as it may seem, as the well water is thickly coated with black oily material which is almost certainly coal tar, and it is well known that coal tar (or *pix carbonis* in technical terminology) according to the *British Pharmaceutical Codex*, 'is used in the treatment of pruritus, psoriasis, eczema, and other skin affections'. In this context it is of interest that the water has been tried at various times in the skin department of the Edinburgh Royal Infirmary. Tradition has it that the well first sprang from oil brought from Mount Sinai, but the more likely, if mundane, explanation is that the oily material seeps into the water from a coal seam.

Healing wells, of course, were not confined to north of the Tweed. Both Wales and England had their quota. In *The Holy Wells of Wales*, Francis Jones records that in the preparation of what is regarded as the standard work on the subject he studied 1179 wells, 370 of which are described exclusively as healing wells. In an analysis of 229 of these, he gives the following list of healing attributes: 78 for eyes, 52 for rheumatism, 47 for skin diseases, 26 for warts, 12 for lameness, 12 for fractures and sprains, and 2 for cancer. This priority for eyes he interestingly links up with Aristotle's comment that the Celts had a custom of 'plunging their newborn children into a cold river'. At the beginning of this century, he records, the people of Rhaeadar in Radnorshire were still bathing the eyes of their babies in the Fair Well, adding: 'I have had the pleasure of speaking to many people who were bathed in that well as children'.

Another well-known well was St Tegla's Well in Clwyd, particularly renowned for the treatment of epilepsy: so much so that this disease became known, and is still known in certain parts of the Principality, as St Tegla's disease. These wells shared with the Celtic wells of the Highlands and Western Isles the ceremonial encircling of the well by the patient, but improved upon it by the addition of the pagan rite, which was retained into the Christian era, of a cock or hen carried round the well and then taken into the neighbouring church where, as part of the cure, the patient spent the night, having deposited his offering of fourpence on the shrine. If the bird died before dawn, the patient would

The Balm Well of St Catherine's Chapel at Grace Mount, near Liberton. *By courtesy of the Wellcome Trustees.*

recover because his disease had been transferred to the stricken fowl.

Today the best known of the Welsh holy wells is St Winifred's Well at Holywell in Flintshire, which within living memory was being boosted as the 'English Lourdes'. So esteemed was it at one time that in 1686 James II and his consort visited it to seek the help of the patron saint in alleviating their infertility. Whether *post hoc* or *propter hoc*, a son, to achieve fame as the Old Pretender, was born two years later. As Francis Jones aptly inquires: 'Is it to this Welsh well that history owes the Old Pretender?' The fee paid by the Royal pair for this 'consultation' was a curious mixture of the macabre and the practical: part of the dress worn by Mary Queen of Scots at her execution, and £30 for the upkeep of the chapel.

In England perhaps the best known was, and is, that at Walsingham, famed for its ability to relieve disorders of the stomach. Equally well known was the Chalice Well at Glastonbury, which leapt to fame in 1750 as a result of one Matthew Chancellor, who had suffered from asthma for nigh on thirty years, dreaming that the waters of the Chalice Well would cure him. Tradition has it that he drank a quarter of a pint on three successive Sundays and was cured. Be that as it may, the story spread and by 1752, 10,000 visitors were pouring into Glastonbury to sample the water. Sad to tell, as it is recorded, this 'celebrity continued until someone overdid the drinking and died there'. A fate, or near-fate, not unknown today in developed as well as developing countries (to use current jargon) among those who still believe that if one pill does you good, ten will do you much more good. Another well-known one in the West Country was St Madran's Well in Cornwall.

Of the many histories attached to these healing wells, not the least interesting is that of the holy well at North Marston in Buckinghamshire. Sir John Schorne, who was rector from 1290 to 1314 and who acquired ecclesiastical fame by confining the Devil in a boot, enhanced his reputation by blessing a local chalybeate well and thereby endowing it with healing powers. So high was his reputation that on his death North Marston became a centre of pilgrimage. Such was its popularity and thereby its resulting wealth, that it aroused the jealousy of the Dean of Windsor who petitioned the Pope for the removal of Schorne's bones to St George's Chapel.

This stopped the pilgrimages but did not affect the popularity of the well and, according to one modern historian, 'Well into the present century sufferers from gout and rheumatism were still taking the waters.' This particular attribute of the water was long recognized by the local doctors and chemists who at one time would slip out in the hours of darkness to collect water from the well, which they then sold to their patients and customers for the relief of their aches and pains. An interesting coincidence is that during the cholera epidemics of last century, North Marston suffered no deaths from the disease though neighbouring villages carried a high mortality rate. Is it possible that the healing well was uncontaminated by local sewerage?

Incidentally, North Marston has another claim to fame in that a local eccentric miser, Neild by name, who died in 1852, left his entire fortune of around £500,000 to Queen Victoria. As there were no known relatives, the Queen felt able to accept the legacy, which she did with gratitude, though, according to one of her biographers, 'The elation of spirit which this munificent addition to her private fortune caused was succeeded by depression on hearing of the death of the Duke of Wellington.' The significance of the gift is indicated by the following excerpt from a letter from King Leopold of the Belgians dated 10 September 1852: 'My Dearest Victoria . . . That Mr Neild should have left this great fortune to you delighted me; it gives the possibility of forming a private fortune for the Royal Family . . .' As the Queen had just embarked on the rebuilding of the recently purchased Balmoral Castle, tradition has it that this munificent gift contributed not a little to the cost. Part of the legacy she used to make provision for Neild's servants, including his housekeeper whom he had apparently completely ignored in his will, and to restore the chancel of North Marston Church where Neild is buried.

It is easy to scoff at these healing wells and to wax cynical about the way the Christian Church manipulated them and incorporated them into its practices as a means of bridging the gulf between paganism and Christianity, not to mention the oft-time sordid financial racket into which they developed. But they do represent an interesting and, on the whole, beneficial transition from the empirical, trial-by-error methods of therapy of our primitive ancestors to the carefully controlled spa therapy of today. Abused they may have been, but what beneficial procedure, particularly in the search for health and the alleviation of disease, has not been abused all down the ages, whether by Church or Medicine, unqualified quack or orthodox practitioner? They did at least provide solace, a far from unimportant healing virtue in the days when life was hard and death an even more threatening menace than it is today, and when chronic crippling disease was all too often the prelude to a purgatorial penury ignored by all but the Church.

These wells that healed cannot be ignored. They undoubtedly subserved a useful therapeutic function. Whether this was achieved by physical or psychological means is of secondary consideration. When mankind had nothing better to offer, they allowed many an afflicted human being to lead a fuller, more contented life – and, as has already been noted, the cure was never worse than the disease, which was, and is, more than can be said of many forms of therapy.

3

British spas

The practice of using natural mineral waters therapeutically by internal and external application on anything like a co-ordinated scale came to Britain from the Continent around the middle of the sixteenth century. Initially the treatment had little scientific basis, consisting merely of simple immersion in baths of mineral water, and the drinking of it – often in heroic amounts. One case is recorded of a distinguished visitor who began with seven pints a day, increased the intake by one pint each day until a maximum of fourteen pints daily was reached, and then reduced it by a pint a day to the original level. Other cases have been recorded when as much as a couple of gallons a day were quaffed in the search for health. Gradually doctors adopted a more rational approach, as exemplified by the writings of leading spa physicians such as Dr William Oliver (of biscuit fame) in Bath, and the report of Dr John Elliott, in 1781, systematically describing all the mineral waters of the country.

Meanwhile the social aspects had been developing. As it has been put, 'The annual visit to a spa was the forerunner of the summer holiday.' By the end of the seventeenth century many northern families went to Buxton and Harrogate, while the Court and London society flocked to Tunbridge Wells until the following century when Bath took its place. Typical of this attitude to spas are the comments of Defoe in 1722: 'The coming to the Well is a mere matter of custom; some drink, more do not, and few drink physically.' Equally typical is the Rev. A. Carlyle's opinion, expressed in 1763, that Harrogate 'was very pleasant, for there was a constant succession of good company, and the best entertainment of any watering-place in Britain, at the least expense'.

It was towards the middle of the nineteenth century that the modern concept of a spa, with a mainly medical outlook gradually appeared, characterized by the substitution of a more scientific basis of practice for the earlier empiricism, and the broadening of the treatment given. Prominent among those who furthered this gradual evolution of our spas was Dr Samuel Hyde (1849–1900) of Buxton, who was largely responsible for the founding, in 1896, of the British Balneological and Climatological Society. This brought together all the leading spa doctors in the country, allowing a free exchange of views and stimulating research into the methods of improving the standards of therapy. Thus, much was done to incorporate into spa therapy the principles of hydrotherapy, the use of exercises and the use of electrotherapy.

Relative to its size, Britain has its fair share of mineral springs, and around the middle of last century there were some thirty places that claimed to be spas. There was, of course, no official classification or registration, as there was on the Continent, and any owner of a mineral spring could describe it as a spa and make whatever claims he liked for it. In some cases these claims and the accompanying developments would be made by individual owners or local residents. In others the 'spa' would be taken over by the local authority or civic authority, or a group of doctors would be the developers.

Although the primary concern of a spa was its healing waters, other factors came into the picture. As *The Spa in Medical Practice*, a report of a committee of the British Medical Association, noted in 1964: 'Although the sites of the spas were first determined by

A painting by William Hoare showing 'Dr Oliver and Mr Peirce, Physician and Surgeon, examining patients afflicted with paralysis, rheumatism and leprosy. Anno 1742.' *Royal National Hospital for Rheumatic Diseases, Bath.*

the presence of mineral springs, it is fortunate that most of the places which have survived as centres of treatment have other attributes such as attractive scenery, historic associations, and are situated at a convenient distance from industrial areas. Indeed these are some of the reasons that they continue to flourish. These natural assets have been enhanced by the skilful laying out of parks and gardens, the provision of residential accommodation in hospitals, convalescent homes and hotels and the construction of adequate therapy departments.'

Not the least of the factors that weighed in the balance in deciding the future prosperity of a spa, was making accessible to the public such isolated spots as Llandrindod Wells in Central

Wales and Strathpeffer in the north of Scotland, and here the development of our modern railway system played an important part. By thus, literally, reducing the length of the journey from days to hours, these delightfully situated spas took on a new lease of life that carried them well into the present century as active centres of the healing art.

The importance attached to spas in the Victorian era is indicated by the fact that in 1889 the council of the Royal Medical and Chirurgical Society resolved, 'that a scientific committee be appointed for the purpose of investigating questions of importance, in reference to the climatology and balneology of Great Britain, and to report thereon to the Council from time to time'. And a high-powered committee it was, its eighteen members including many of the leading consultant physicians of the day. The committee's report was published in two volumes.

Volume I, published in 1895, dealt with 'the climates of the south of England and the chief medical springs of Great Britain'. In the course of this it is noted that, 'When the baths and inland watering-places of Great Britain are marshalled before us for inspection, their number appears but small as compared to the abundance of similar provisions of nature existing upon the continent of Europe. However, in their relatively small array, some resorts can be ranked of first importance.' On the other hand, it is pointed out, 'It could hardly be expected that, where there is such a comparative paucity of choice, we should find representatives of all the kinds of thermal and mineral waters which determine the existence of large resorts among the continental peoples. Whilst Great Britain possesses some excellent thermal waters, none of them contain any such powerful mineral constituents as are found at Carlsbad, Aix-la-Chapelle, or Wiesbaden; neither do we possess any springs of a strong chalybeate quality, such, for example, as those of Schwalbach, Spa, Pyrmont, and St Moritz; nor alkaline sources such as those of Vichy and Contrexéville; neither have we any waters in which excess of carbon dioxide produces natural effervescence, as at Homburg and other places. There are, however, included in our list sulphur springs of marked strength, besides saline springs and natural brines of no mean value, in several cases associated with the presence of iron.'

The spas, or 'mineral springs', the term used in the report, visited and reported on by members of the committee, consisted of Bath, Buxton, Matlock, Bakewell, Stoney Middleton, Harrogate, Askern Spa, Droitwich, Nantwich, Stafford, Saltburn-on-Sea, Woodhall Spa, Ashby-De-La-Zouche, Leamington, Cheltenham, Tunbridge Wells, Strathpeffer, Moffat, Llandrindod, Llanwrtyd, Llangammarch, and Builth – twenty-two in all.

The thoroughness with which the investigation was carried out is indicated by the comment that, 'Beyond the questions of the temperature and chemical constitution of waters, questions of climate, of relative elevation of site, and, to no small extent, of social arrangements also go far to determine the usefulness of particular inland watering-places.' Other factors taken into consideration were 'the use of accessory treatments, by artificial modifications of the mineral waters, or by the addition of waters from other sources, as well as in the form of mechanical or electrical therapeutical devices'.

In this context it is of more than passing interest that the distinguished Victorian physicians felt it necessary to make the following comments:

> 'There also arises a question of some delicacy – namely, that of discipline and regimen. In the taking of baths and waters more has to be regarded than their simple influence, and there can be no doubt that the institution of strict discipline, in respect of hours of rising and of resting, in respect of exercise and of dietary, contributes very largely to the beneficial effects of a course. To this end the co-operation of the medical man and of his patients is necessary. Very probably our insular freedom is chargeable with some neglect in this matter. There is perhaps too little general concert of

> opinion and action among the medical men in our bath places, and still more a reluctance on the part of the patients to submit in England to a degree of restraint which they would readily accept at Carlsbad or Vichy.'

The second volume, which came out in 1902, is devoted to 'the climates of London and of the central and northern portions of England, together with those of Wales and Ireland'. It includes references to a number of mineral springs, 'more of antiquarian interest', including Flitwick and Shearsby (the former in Bedfordshire, the latter in Leicestershire), Shap, and Trefriw in the valley of the Conway. There is a separate chapter on 'The Mineral Springs of Ireland', written by Sir Norman Moore, as distinguished as a medical historian (with a special interest in Irish history) as a physician and President of the Royal College of Physicians of London in his time. He introduces his chapter by saying: 'The mineral springs of Ireland are numerous and valuable, but their conveniences seem to have been but little developed since the time of Rutty' – a doctor who wrote a book on the mineral springs of Great Britain and Ireland in 1757. The only one Sir Norman considers worthy of consideration is that at Lisdoonvarna in County Clare.

His account is far from impressive. While fairly non-committal about its four springs, with the possible exception of the sulphur one, he obviously finds it hard to say anything complimentary about the general lay-out. Thus, 'There are three or four hotels besides many houses in which lodgings can be obtained', but 'the standard of comfort is not at present very high, nor are there any amusements. A good performance on the Irish pipes, and occasional fiddlers versed in the pleasing native music are the sole representatives of the concerts of foreign spas.' He also notes that the local doctors were 'unanimous' about the efficacy of the spa in 'the conditions due to alcoholism and to sedentary life'.

From the beginning of this century the popularity of British spas began to decline, though only gradually. Ancillary forms of treatment, such as electrotherapy, were introduced and an almost infinite variety of different douches and sprays were imported from the Continent. They therefore still remained an essential feature of the British medical scene until the First World War.

In 1918 many of them were still viable and in existence, and in a book published in 1919 (*Spas and Health Resorts of the British Isles*), Dr T. D. Luke, who describes himself as physician-in-charge, Peebles Hydropathic, lists nineteen: Bath, Harrogate, The Matlocks, Buxton, Nantwich, Woodhall Spa, Droitwich, Leamington, Malvern, Tunbridge Wells, Cheltenham, Trefriw, Llandrindod Wells, Llangammarch Wells, Llanwrtyd Wells, Peebles, Bridge of Allan, Moffat, and Strathpeffer. In addition he mentions a host of 'minor spas and wells'. In view of what Sir Norman Moore had to say about Irish spas in 1902, it is of interest to note what Dr Luke has to say about them: 'Of mineral springs Lisdoonvarna is perhaps the most outstanding . . . It is small but quite the most popular spa in Ireland.' Others he mentions are Lucan in County Kildare, Mallow in County Cork, Castle Connell in Limerick, and Ballynahinch in Ulster, adding, however, that 'none of these receives much attention at the present time'. 'St Anne's Hill Hydro in Cork' is described as 'deserving of mention, as it is one of the very oldest of such establishments in the kingdom.' It is of sociological, if not medical, interest that the book is introduced by a slashing attack on the standards of British hotels.

Throughout the 1918–1939 era the decline slowly continued, partly as a result of failure of the nation to recognize the extent of the rheumatic problem, partly as a result of the medical profession finding it so difficult to adapt to the new scientific winds of change.

The outbreak of war in 1939, followed by the introduction of the National Health Service in 1948, seemed to many to 'toll the knell of parting day' for British spas, but there was life in them still. On the introduction of the Service, the spa hospitals with their thousand or so beds were taken over and transferred to the

Minister of Health. Unfortunately the spa establishments themselves were not, and from this splitting of function has arisen many of the troubles of the present day. In certain spas, such as Bath, Droitwich and Leamington, the Ministry continued to pay for National Health Service patients who were treated in them, but there was no statutory obligation to do this, and, when a misguided medical profession decided that all the benefits of a spa could be obtained in the hydrotherapy department of a National Health Service hospital, not unnaturally the powers that be took the line of least financial resistance and gradually reduced what amounted to a subsidy to the old spas.

For a time, however, spas, though in diminishing number, continued as an integral part of the medical life of the country, as exemplified by the appearance in 1951 of a handbook entitled *The Spa in Medical Practice* prepared by a committee set up by the Council of the British Medical Association under the chairmanship of Lord Horder, that most versatile and shrewd of inter-war London consultants. The committee was set up on the suggestion of the Association's Spa Practitioners Group Committee as general practitioners were finding 'some difficulty in obtaining authoritative information about the medical treatment available at British spas'.

When a second edition appeared in 1964 it carried the following preface: 'The practice of medicine at the spas continues to be profoundly affected, like other branches of medicine, by the steady advance in knowledge. The wind of change during the twelve years since this booklet was first produced is indicated in small measure by the fact that its instigator, the Spa Practitioners Group Committee of the British Medical Association, no longer exists. Its interests have been absorbed into the wider field of the Physical Medicine Group Committee. This change is indicative of the close co-operation that now exists between consultants in Physical Medicine and the Spa Practitioners.' The only spas listed in the booklet were Bath, Buxton, Cheltenham, Droitwich, Leamington, and Woodhall Spa. In other words there were only six spas left in the United Kingdom. Fourteen years later there is only one – Leamington.

The reasons for this sombre state of affairs are not far to seek, and are discussed in subsequent chapters of this book. Meanwhile all that need be said here is that all of the spas in this attenuated list are viable and that there are no good reasons why they should not be revived – to the benefit of the hundreds of thousands of crippled and rheumatic citizens in our midst. They are all spas that have healed in the past and there is no reason why they should not continue their mission of healing.

4

London spas of yesteryear

The eighteenth century was the hey-day of the commercialization of spas. Bath, Epsom and Tunbridge Wells had set the fashion, and the entrepreneurs were quick off the mark in making use of a multiplicity of London wells and springs to attract the inhabitants of the capital. Pleasure gardens became all the rage. Not all were associated with wells or springs, but in those that were the medicinal attraction of the wells, with their claims to fame backed up by medical commendations of doubtful origin and validity, was enhanced by all the sales' ingenuity that showmen have shown down the ages. The interest of the medical profession in these spas was relatively slight. The hey-day of spas as a serious contribution to medicine was yet to come.

Islington Spa, or the New Tunbridge Wells, as it was also known on account of the similarity of its waters to those of Tunbridge Wells, was typical of these London spas. A near neighbour of the much better known Sadler's Wells, with which it was often confused, the chalybeate spring on which it was based was discovered around 1680. By 1685 it was being advertised for its 'sweet gardens and arbours of pleasure'. While, according to Warwick Wroth, in his delightful *The London Pleasure Gardens of the Eighteenth Century*, 'The company was extraordinarily mixed,' noting that, 'Virtue and vice, fashion and the negation of fashion had all their representatives.' A doctor attended the spa to give advice to the water drinkers, 'not a few of whom', according to Wroth, 'came for the purpose of benefiting their health.' One of its early advocates was Lady Mary Wortley Montagu, though she did admit that excess of the waters made her drowsy.

It had its ups and downs, reaching its peak of popularity when it was patronized in 1723 by George III's two daughters, Princess Amelia and Princess Caroline. The last to attempt to revive it was a local surgeon called Malloy, who, in 1844, by printed circulars, invited invalids to drink the waters for an annual subscription of one guinea, or sixpence a visit. By mid-century, however, it had ceased to exist, though at the end of the century the coping stone of the proprietor's house in Lloyd's Row bore the superscription: ISLINGTON SPA OR NEW TUNBRIDGE WELLS. This final remnant survived until the Second World War when it disappeared among the rubble of London bombing.

The neighbouring Sadler's Wells, so named after the enterprising surveyor who rediscovered them, had a much shorter history as a spa. The original wells, which belonged to St John's Priory, Clerkenwell, fell into disuse after the dissolution of the monasteries. They were rediscovered quite accidentally in 1683 by workmen in the gardens of Sadler's Music House. Sadler, with a shrewd eye to business, had the water analysed by Dr Thomas Guidot, an authority on mineral waters. According to Guidot's report, as summarized by Wroth, the water was 'ferruginous chalybeate, akin to the waters of Tunbridge Wells, though not tasting so strongly of steel and having more of a nitrous sulphur about it. Being neither offensive nor unpleasant to taste, a man was able to drink more of it than of any other liquor. It might be taken with a few carraway comfits, some elecampane, or a little preserved angelica to comfort the stomach. A glass of Rhenish or white wine might also accompany the tonic, and habitual smokers would find it very convenient to take a pipe after drinking.'

On the receipt of this report Sadler was off the mark like a shot with his publicity. So successful was he that Epsom and Tunbridge Wells were stung into producing a tract protesting against this 'horrid plot' and asking whether it was possible for water from such a source to 'bee as effectual as our wonder-working fountains that taste of cold iron, and breathe pure nitre and sulphur'. Whether *post hoc* or *propter hoc*, Sadler's Wells rapidly lost its popularity in spite of Sadler's claim that its water was effectual in 'curing all hectic and hypochondriacal distempers', and by the turn of the century water-drinking had ceased, leaving Sadler's Wells henceforth in the hands of the historian of the theatre and music.

The grandiloquently entitled London Spa's only claim to mention is that it was officially opened, in 1685, in the grounds of the Fountain Inn in Finsbury, by Robert Boyle, the distinguished chemist and one of the founders of the Royal Society, who apparently was of the opinion that its waters were 'the strongest and very best of these late found out medicinal waters'. The waters, however, sadly failed to compete with mine host's home-brewed ale, and by the mid-1750s the Inn had reverted to its original role as a tavern.

St Chad's Well, King's Cross, was a popular resort in the latter part of the eighteenth century, among its patrons being John Abernethy, the famous surgeon. It lost popularity after the turn of the century but was renovated by a new proprietor in 1837, who recommended the waters, which contained large amounts of sodium sulphate (Glauber's salt) and magnesia, as a universal medicine, 'actively purgative, mildly tonic and powerfully diuretic'. The pump-room was opened at 5 am, and the price of admission was threepence, or one guinea a year. It finally ended its days making room for the excavations for the new Metropolitan Railway in the 1860s.

Bagnigge Wells, now buried under King's Cross Station, owes its entry to this list of London spas of yesteryear to somewhat similar circumstances to those which led to the discovery of Epsom as a spa – the acute observation of a man of the land. The wells received their name from Bagnigge House, the building in

Sadler's Wells in 1792, and as it was before 1765. *From a drawing by R. C. Andrews.*

whose grounds they were discovered and which was reputed to have been Nell Gwynne's summer residence. Its tenant in 1757, a keen and obviously observant gardener, found that the more he watered his plants with the water drawn from a well in the garden, the less they seemed to thrive. His curiosity aroused, he asked Dr John Bevis, a physician and astronomer and a Fellow of the Royal Society, to analyse it. His report showed it to be a chalybeate (i.e. iron-containing) water, while the water of a neighbouring well, sunk some forty yards away, was found to have cathartic properties.

The tenant immediately saw the commercial possibilities and by early 1759 had opened the house and grounds to the public, charging threepence for the privilege of drinking the water, or half a guinea for the season. The following year Dr Bevis backed him up with a pamphlet in which the chalybeate water was described as having 'an agreeable and sprightly sub-acid tartness', and as 'apt to communicate a kind of giddiness with an amazing flow of spirits and afterwards a propensity to sleep if exercise be not interposed'. The cathartic water was said to leave a 'distinguishable brackish bitterness on the palate' and three half-pints were 'sufficient for most people'.

Such were the waters, fed into a dome-shaped building known as The Temple, that for the next forty years or so, some hundreds of visitors were to be found drinking in the morning, followed by early breakfast. Stronger alcoholic refreshments, as well as tea, were also available in the surrounding gardens, to which attractions such as bowling greens and skittle-alleys were added. After the turn of the century, however, its popularity gradually waned, and it finally closed down in 1841, having changed hands several times.

King's Cross was not the only railway station to be associated with these eighteenth century London spas. Its near neighbour, St Pancras Station, occupies the site of another well-known spa: Pancras Wells. Its waters, according to handbills published in 1697, had been found 'from long experience' to be 'a powerful antidote against rising of the vapours, also against the stone and gravel'. 'It likewise', it was also claimed, 'cleanses the body and sweetens the blood and is a general and sovereign help to nature.' And all for threepence, which included admission to the surrounding extensive tea-gardens, or six shillings for a dozen bottles from a goldsmith of the name of Richard Bristow.

Nearby, between Pancras Wells and the Adam and Eve Tea-Gardens at the north end of Tottenham Court Road, was what was known as the Cold Bath. Discovered around the turn of the seventeenth century it was situated in pleasant gardens. An ad-

A view of Bagnigge Wells Gardens 'drawn on ye spot'. *Frontispiece for the 'Sunday Ramble'.*

vertisement of 1785 described it as in fine order for the reception of ladies and gentlemen, its water being 'serviceable to persons suffering from nervous disorders and dejected spirits'. Earlier, an enterprising owner described it as the 'Cockney Pool of Bethesda' and drew attention to the fact that the infirm could be lowered into it in a chair. A commendable, if hitherto ignored, pioneer effort to help the disabled in our midst – and long before the creation of a Minister for the Disabled.

Although most of these London spas were on the north side of the Thames, with a particular conglomeration around the Fleet which thus became known as the River of Wells, the south side of the river had its quota. Three of these are particularly deserving of notice.

Dulwich Spa, which dates from the middle of the eighteenth century, was discovered quite accidentally while workmen were digging for household water. By a curious coincidence Professor John Martyn, F.R.S., a distinguished botanist and pharmacist, was standing by at the time. As the water bubbled up he tasted it and decided that it was worth analysing. This was duly done and the results, reported to the Royal Society, indicated that it was a new medicinal well. Until towards the end of the century the spa flourished, the water not only being drunk on the spot, but also supplied regularly to St Bartholomew's Hospital. It is of passing interest that after its demise as a spa the building was occupied by Lord Chancellor Thurlow for a time, and then used as a school, one of whose pupils was Lord Byron.

Lambeth Wells were situated on what is now the famous Lambeth Walk. There were two wells, and their purgative waters were supplied to St Thomas's Hospital and elsewhere at a penny a quart. The poor had it free, while threepence was charged for admission to the spa: this included drinking the water and listening to the music. Opened towards the end of the seventeenth century, it began to lose its attraction with the advent of the neighbouring St George's Spaw and it closed down around the middle of the eighteenth century. Its Great Room, in which dances and concerts had been held, was taken over by the Methodists but, according to Wroth, 'The preacher being disturbed greatly in his enthusiastic harangues was obliged to quit.' An unusual experience for the militant Methodists of those days.

St George's Spaw, situated within half a mile of Lambeth Wells, began life as the Dog and Duck, a small inn which derived its name from the local sport of hunting duck with spaniels. In the vicinity were mineral springs which, the proprietor noticed, produced a profuse growth of water violets. They were found to have an aperient action, but the water does not seem to have been advertised until around 1730, when the humble inn changed its name to St George's Spaw. This social uplift was largely the result of commendation of the water by physicians as eminent as Dr John Fothergill, according to whom, it 'would cure most cutaneous disorders, and be useful for keeping the body cool, and preventing cancerous affections'. Others recommended it (fourpence a gallon at the pump, or twelve bottles for twelvepence) for gout, stone, sore eyes and the King's evil, and among those who bought it was that gouty, if beautiful, termagant, Sarah Duchess of Marlborough.

Under this illustrious umbrella the spa flourished during the latter part of the eighteenth century, the *St James's Chronicle* ranking the water with that of Buxton, Cheltenham and Tunbridge. Such indeed was its fame that Dr Samuel Johnson, who is on record as declaiming that, 'Medicated baths can be no better than warm water; their only effect can be that of tepid moisture,' recommended its water to Mrs Thrale.

As so often in such concerns, financial success went to the heads of the owners and the spa gradually declined, becoming what Wroth in precise Victorian language describes as 'a place of assignation and the haunt of "the riff-raff and scum of the town"'. It finally ended its variegated career in 1811, when it was pulled down for the building of Bethlem Hospital. A footnote that will be appreciated by the cynics in our midst is that in 1856, Dr William Rendle, the Southwark antiquary who practised there for nearly half a century and was the Officer of Health for the parish of St George's, Southwark, had the water analysed, as a result of which his verdict was that it was 'a decidedly unsafe water'.

Historical continuity demands the mention of one more of these London spas of yesteryear: Beulah Spaw in Upper Norwood. With its buildings designed by Decimus Burton, who laid out Hyde Park and was the architect who rebuilt Tunbridge Wells between 1828 and 1848, and its water shown by Michael Faraday to have a high magnesium sulphate (Epsom salts) content, and its twenty-five acres of beautifully laid out gardens (complete with *camera obscura*, maze and the like), for nigh on a quarter of a century, from 1831 to 1854, it was one of London's foremost pleasure resorts. Among its devotees was Mrs Fitzherbert, on whose recommendation the Duke of Gloucester sampled its waters to 'stimulate his jaded liver'.

Alas, its grounds are now typical suburbia, but one relic of its hey-day still exists – or at least did exist at the end of 1975. Known as Tivoli Lodge, and described by Peterborough in *The Daily Telegraph* as 'one of South London's most historic buildings', it was one of the two lodges at the entrance to the spa and served as the box office and reception hall. According to *The Daily Telegraph* of 4 November 1975, 'It has been wrecked by vandals. Empty since July, it has had every window smashed, its interior plundered and obscenities scrawled all around.' The Norwood Society is pressing the local authorities to maintain it but, like so many such moves for the preservation of our heritage, the fate of this surviving remnant of the London spas is in the balance.

It was not only the metropolis itself that had its spas. In a spa-conscious age it was surrounded by a circle of spas, from Totteridge, Cheshunt, Barnet and Welwyn in the north, to Richmond and Cobham in the west, Epsom in the south and Woodford and Wanstead in the east. None of these, with the exception of Epsom, achieved prolonged fame, but some of them, such as Barnet and Cheshunt in Hertfordshire and Wanstead in Essex, had their day of popularity, largely patronized by the inhabitants of London; hence the justification for including them in this chapter.

Such was the reputation of Barnet in the seventeenth century that, according to the Rev. Thomas Fullerton in his *Worthies of England* (1662), 'The catalogue of the cures done by this spring amounteth to a great number; insomuch that there is hope, in the process of time, that the waters rising here will repair the blood shed by, and save as many lives as were lost in, the fatal battle of Barnet.' Samuel Pepys, who sampled the water twice, was not quite so enthusiastic when he found that after drinking five glasses on one visit he had to dismount seven or eight times on the way home, and then spent a restless night, sweating 'worse and worse' until he 'melted almost to water'. There was certainly no doubt about the potency of the water. Its reputation died hard, and as late as 1800 the Rev. W. M. Trinder, M.D., published a pamphlet entitled *The Barnet Well Water*.

The Cheshunt, or Northaw, Well owed its popularity to James I of England. In view of its proximity to his palace of Theobalds, the well became known to, and popular with, the members of his court, and in 1660 Charles II gave permission for it to be known as the King's Well. It was a chalybeate well.

The Wanstead Spa had its career cut short by the drying up of its well. At one time a fashionable village, Wanstead had every prospect of developing into a really popular spa. Writing in 1619 to Sir Dudley Carleton (later Viscount Dorchester), John Chamberlain, the well-known letter writer of those days, waxed eloquent about 'a new spa, or spring of that nature, found lately about Wanstead; and much running there is to it daily, both by lords and ladies and other great company, so that they have almost drawn it dry already; and, if it should hold on, it would put down the waters at Tunbridge.'

Alas, these dreams were not to be fulfilled. The water disappeared entirely, the explanation given being, not excessive use, but draining operations in the vicinity. That this is the probable explanation of why Essex lost its fashionable spa is supported by the author of H.M. Stationery Office's booklet, *Wanstead Park*: 'In view of the recurring problem of maintaining the water level in the Park's ornamental waters, this explanation of Wanstead's failure to develop as a spa is perfectly credible.'

The story of these London spas of yesteryear may be more a contribution to social, than medical, history, but they do constitute a direct link between the holy or healing wells of the Middle Ages and the modern spas that were to develop during the latter half of the great Victorian era. It may at times have been a tenuous thread, but it did persist, illustrating the continuing faith of both the laity and doctors in spas that heal. 'Men may come and men may go, But I go on for ever' sang Tennyson's brook, and so it might also be said of the healing waters that gush forth from the bowels of the earth. In spite of all the antagonism of modern science they still exert their soothing influence on many of the aches and pains to which man is heir.

5

Bath Spa

'Narrow minds will ever have narrow views. The corporation of *Bath* seems to have forgot that the ease and plenty they now enjoy, and to which their fathers were strangers are owing to their Waters; and that an improvement upon their Baths would, by bringing a greater concourse of company to their town, perpetuate these blessings to them and their posterity . . . It is to be hoped, there are still some among us, whose exalted station, superior sense and public spirit, will be sufficient to interest the legislature in an affair which is truly national, that the public may no longer suffer from the private claims, sordid passions, or selfish views of any particular set of men. Those salutary Springs are the gift of heaven, of such consequence to the health of individuals, as to claim the particular protection of the public . . . In an age like this, when such sums are expended by private persons upon works of magnificence and decoration; when such considerable aids are granted for the utility and encouragement of commerce; and our administration seems so well disposed to consult, and promote, the wellfare of the Commonwealth; we have reason to believe, that some attention will be paid to those fountains flowing with health, which at a very moderate expense, might be so improved as to become the greatest boast, ornament, and blessing of these kingdoms.'

So wrote Tobias Smollett, M.D., in 1752 in *An Essay on the External Use of Water*. Two-and-a-quarter centuries later – on 3 December 1976 – at 5 pm (or 17.00 hours in modern terminology) the key was turned in the door of the Spa Treatment Centre and for an indefinite period – for ever so far as the City Council and the Wiltshire Area Health Authority were concerned – the most historic spa in the United Kingdom closed its hitherto ever-open doors, and the long-suffering (literally and metaphorically) British public was deprived of its healing waters. In the words of Mrs Ida Prins-Buttle, who, as chairman of the Action Committee for Bath Spa Preservation, had fought a gallant rearguard action against this classical example of vandalism and medical stupidity, this was 'the saddest day that Bath has known'.

British Rail still names it Bath Spa – a pathetic reminder of the glory that was Bath. Without its healing waters Bath has not merely been emasculated, it has been petrified just as effectively as was Pompeii by the lava of Vesuvius. The juggernaut of the National Health Service, with the enthusiastic backing of much of the medical profession, has converted Bath into a lifeless museum piece. All, however, is not lost but, before looking into the future, a glance at the past will keep things in perspective.

As a sociological and architectural phenomenon Bath has probably had more written about it than any other city in the country. What tends to be overlooked in most of these writings is that, in the words of the 1976 official guide book to the city, 'The reason for the existence of Bath is water. The whole place has been built because of, and literally on, the only hot mineral springs in Britain . . . The waters are the reason for the legend of Bath's beginning; the reason for the Romans building here their most important bathing establishment in Britain; the reason for the great eighteenth century social life and architectural development; and the reason for the spa today.' If only the City Fathers

The Great Bath of the Roman Baths in Bath. *Bath City Council.*

had read and 'inwardly digested' their own official guide book before they closed the source of their city's glory.

To unravel the spa theme from all its, at times enigmatic, variations is a fascinating study in many facets of human nature and many historical by-ways. Inevitably it all starts with a legend of infinite variety. Essentially, however, it is that Prince Bladud, variously described as a Prince of Wessex, a descendant of Brutus, the son of Lud Hudibras, eighth king of the Britons and (here all the variations are in agreement) the father of King Lear, became an outcast as a result of developing leprosy. Finally he was reduced to becoming a swineherd. To add to his misfortunes, his pigs developed a skin disease – some say leprosy acquired from their keeper. Be that as it may, one day, around 860 B.C., after wallowing in a hot steamy swamp by the banks of the Avon his pigs emerged cured of their skin disease. On the principle that what was good for his pigs might well be good for him – or perhaps in sheer desperation – the stricken Prince plunged into the steaming swamp, and emerged cured of his leprosy. Overjoyed he hurried back to his father's court where he received the traditional welcome of the prodigal son and, when he finally became king, he built a spa at the site of his 'cure' and called it Bladud, from which the modern name of Bath is derived.

Some eight centuries later, in one of those delightful phrases, of which Victorian guide books are such a rich source, 'with the Roman period we pass from the darkness of tradition into historic light'. The Romans, with their traditional interest in baths, were not slow in discovering, and making full use of the hot springs of Bath, and for the next hundred years *Aquae Sulis*, so named after Sul, the Celtic goddess of springs, identified by the Romans with Minerva, thrived as a spa, attracting visitors from all over Roman-occupied Britain as well as the northern provinces of the Empire.

When they finally evacuated Britain the Romans, in the words of a Victorian writer, 'left behind them in the city of Bath a palace of health and luxury unequalled except in Italy' – a statement which anyone who has visited the Roman remains as now presented to the visitor will willingly accept. Even the Pompeiian remains, recently brought so magnificently to the attention of Londoners, scarcely excel them in the vividness with which they recall the great days of a great civilization. Would that the City Fathers of Bath had paid as much attention to the thermal springs committed to their care as they have to these Roman remains.

The next thousand years can be rapidly passed over. The Saxons did their traditional best to exterminate Roman civilization but, following the Norman Conquest, the Church took an interest in the city as a centre of healing based on its thermal springs. Thus, towards the end of the eleventh century a court physician from Tours called John de Villula, who had employed the waters curatively, 'tiring of the profession of medicine', bought the city for 500 marks (£60), took holy orders and in due course became Bishop of Wells, taking up his residence in Bath. It was in his time that the King's Bath was built. His successors maintained the tradition of supervising the care of the sick who came to Bath for its waters, and it was one of these, Reginald Fitzjocelyn, who provided the Hospital of St John, now an almshouse, and one of the most fascinating corners of old Bath. He also built the Cross Bath.

Following this ecclesiastical interregnum, which ended with the dissolution of the monasteries, the hot springs and baths became city property, and what may be described as the modern era of Bath Spa began – to last for more than four centuries until in gross dereliction of duty the City Council followed the example of the Saxon barbarians and deprived the nation of this source of healing waters.

What might be described as the initiation of this modern era was the visit, in 1616, of Queen Anne of Denmark, the consort of James I, seeking relief from her dropsy. It is after her that the Queen's Bath is named. Her successors – Henrietta Maria, Catherine of Braganza, and Mary of Modena, the consorts, respectively, of Charles I, Charles II and James II – all sampled the waters, the last two in the hope that it could cure their infertility, as did Queen Anne in 1702.

With this galaxy of royalty, Bath became an essential part of the social season for the aristocracy, and they, followed by the squirearchy and then the successful merchants and bankers with their socially ambitious spouses, guaranteed that Bath never looked back. Whether they would have continued coming if it had not been for the fortunate, if quite fortuitous, appearance of a unique trio is an open question. The first of these, a Welshman called Richard Nash, who has gone down in history as Beau Nash, arrived in the city as a 29-year-old gambler in 1705. This began a career as social dictator of Bath which, in the words of one commentator, 'lasted more than fifty-five years and ended with an abbey funeral that would have done honour to a royal duke'. The second was a Cornishman, Ralph Allen, who was appointed postmaster of the city in 1710, made a fortune out of Government contracts, and devoted this to buying the neighbouring stone quarries. He further improved his prospects, financial and social, by marrying the illegitimate daughter of General Wade, the bachelor Member of Parliament for Bath. From this strong position he shrewdly decided that the time had come to rebuild Bath and make it one of the show cities of the country. For this purpose he roped in the services of a Yorkshire architect, John Wood who, with his son, was responsible for Queen Square, the Circus, Royal Crescent and the Assembly Rooms (gutted by bombing in one of the Baedeker raids of 1942, but since rebuilt) which initiated a complete rebuilding of the city, that has been described as 'a fantastic achievement of town planning unrivalled anywhere else in Britain, if not in Europe'.

Incidentally, it is of interest that it was around this period that the royal physician recommended that the waters should be drunk, thus giving rise to what became the social ritual of Bath, immortalized by Jane Austen and other writers, and the building of the Pump Room in 1706. Hitherto the waters had largely been used for bathing in.

Inevitably this social microcosm became a magnet that attracted writers, novelists and poets in search of material for their works. A list of them would merely be a list of practically all the great figures in English literature – from Pope to Dickens and Thackeray – but probably the best known are Smollett with *Peregrine Pickle* and *Humphrey Clinker*, and Jane Austen with *Northanger Abbey* and *Persuasion*. Sir Walter Scott was also a visitor, but in childhood, seeking treatment for what he described as his 'much shrunk and contracted' right leg. He spent a year in Bath when he was four years old, and his own account of the visit is of more than passing interest.

The Assembly Rooms, designed by John Wood the Younger, were built between 1769 and 1771 for a total cost of £20,000. *J. Benedict Blathwayt.*

> 'I was in my fourth year when my father was advised that the Bath waters might be of some advantage to my lameness. My affectionate aunt, although such a journey promised to a person of her retired habits anything but pleasure or amusement, undertook as readily to accompany me to the wells of Bladud as if she had expected all the delight that ever the prospect of a watering-place held out to its most impatient visitants . . . At Bath where I lived about a year, I went through all the usual discipline of the pump-room and baths, but I believe without the least advantage to my lameness.'

The connecting link between this social hey-day and the present is the 'Bath Hospital', opened in 1742, largely as the result of the money-raising efforts of Beau Nash, the architectural plans of John Wood and the Bath stone presented by Ralph Allen, with Dr William Oliver, of biscuit fame, as senior physician. William Oliver was a Cornishman who settled in practice in Bath in 1725. His initial success he owed to his fellow-Cornishman, Ralph Allen, but this he would never have achieved had he not been a sound physician as well as, in the words of a contemporary, an 'essentially sensible man, compassionate and benevolent'. His famous 'Bath Olivers' he concocted, in his own words, as 'a nutritious and easily digested food for rheumatic sufferers'. The secret of their unique flavour is said to lie in the making; the ingredients are 'finest flour, pure dairy milk, butter and malt'. Oliver himself made no effort to profit from his biscuits. Shortly before his death he handed over the recipe to Atkins, his coachman, along with one hundred pounds in cash and 'ten sacks of finest wheaten flour'. Atkins opened a small shop on Green Street, Bath, and made a fortune for himself and his descendants.

In the first instance the Bath Hospital was basically a home for 140 patients. Originally they went to the hot springs for their treatment, but in 1830 water was laid on direct from the hot spring to the hospital. The hospital steadily expanded and by 1887, when it was renamed the Royal Mineral Water Hospital, the annual intake of patients was over a thousand. Around the same time – 1885 – over 80,000 'bathers' were recorded in New Royal Baths.

The 1930s, in the ominous words of the two senior physicians to the hospital, writing in 1969, 'saw a change of attitude in Bath as therapy came to be used more critically'. They add: 'To signify this the name of the hospital was changed to the Royal National Hospital for Rheumatic Diseases . . . the "waters" became just a part, although an important one, in a programme of rehabilitation.'

Meanwhile the Spa Treatment Centre, established in 1869 and owned by the city, which dealt only with paying patients, was being modernized. With the advent of the National Health

Service in 1948, the Centre was made available for hospital out-patients, as well as private patients. The city's spa department was reimbursed by the National Health Service, but it ran the Centre deliberately at a slight loss as its contribution to the amenities of the city. Gradually, over the subsequent years the number of private patients steadily decreased. In the 1960s the hospital, which had had one wing destroyed in one of the Baedeker raids of 1942, was reconstructed at a cost of £300,000.

Meanwhile plans were going ahead for the building of a new general hospital, the Royal United Hospital, at Combe Park on the heights overlooking Bath: possibly an excellent bracing site for a hospital, but just as awkward a place as could have been chosen for elderly rheumatic patients to get to, especially in view of the hopelessly inadequate public bus service that now characterizes Bath as well as most of the country. What brought matters to a head was the decision to open a large hydrotherapy department in this new hospital. This included a large treatment pool, or bath, heated from the heating system of the hospital. This new development meant a diminishing number of National Health Service patients using the Spa Treatment Centre, which since the inception of the National Health Service had been carrying out around 40,000 treatments a year. This in turn placed a heavier financial burden on the Bath City Council, due to the reduction in the financial contribution from the Wiltshire Area Health Authority, and in December 1975 the Bath City Council gave one year's notice terminating the agreement between the city and the Health Authority under which the Spa Centre had been run. And close it did, as already recorded.

It is a pathetic, indeed tragic, epilogue to a history of healing waters stretching back some two thousand years. As one of the leading Bath physicians has put it, 'Whatever economic and social changes overtake us, the hot waters of Bath will continue to flow half a million gallons daily at a temperature of 49° C. (120° F.), as they always have done. And as long as they flow there will continue to be those who ask: "Couldn't I be helped by treatment at Bath?".' The answer is in the affirmative in the case of many patients.

The present position is not only tragic; it is also ludicrous. Here is half a million gallons of hot water going to waste in central Bath in these days of appeals for conservation of energy, while expensive fuel has to be burned to heat water on its outskirts to carry out the function that the naturally hot water would do just as well – if not better. In addition, the senior citizens of Bath who could pop into the Spa Treatment Centre during the course of a morning's or afternoon's shopping, have now to wend their weary way on their stiffening limbs by an inadequate bus service to the heights (760 feet) of the city for their treatment – an expedition which may well take the greater part of the day.

On top of all this is the loss of the medicinal value of the water. Up to the time it closed the Spa Centre was issuing a leaflet, presumably approved by the local medical fraternity, claiming that the 'water piped direct from the Hot Springs is used in a variety of treatments which are now enjoying a new lease of life because of their unique relaxing and beneficial effect', adding, 'Many doctors are enthusiastic about the contribution that thermal mineral waters can make to the alleviation of rheumatic, arthritic and similar conditions.'

Why has such a state of affairs arisen? The simple answer is lack of foresight on the part of the Bath City Council as the responsible authority for the Spa Treatment Centre, and lack of interest – if not positive obstruction – on the part of the medical profession. If, in 1945, the City Council had had the foresight to plan the renovation of the Treatment Centre, it would still be a going concern. But little, if anything, was done – partly, to be fair, because of lack of constructive ideas and support from the local medical profession.

The whole concept of the replanning and renovation of the historic central part of Bath, which includes the baths, should have been based on them. The Pump Room Hotel, for instance, should never have been allowed to be demolished. But, for all practical purposes, nothing was done. All the emphasis was on architectural preservation and renovation, overlooking entirely the fact that without its unique hot springs, Bath would lose much of its major claims as a tourist centre.

Typical of the attitude of the local consultants are the ominous concluding sentences of an article two of them wrote in 1969: 'Today the focus of interest has already turned away from the concept of the spa to the study and relief of disease within the context of the health service. The stage is now set for a future of increasing application of science and technology to many aspects of rheumatology. The tools and methods may be new, but the principles of clinical practice will, we trust, continue to maintain all that is best of the old and honourable standards of medicine in Bath.'

Yet it is one of these same consultants who writes in 1975: 'It is painfully apparent that hydrotherapy and spa treatment in general has been much neglected in this country . . . Hydrotherapy and spa treatment could play a much greater role in Britain than is generally recognized. It would indeed be tragic if this recognition finally came when all of our spas had been dismantled.'

And so we come full circle to the present state of affairs when, somewhat belatedly and on a disturbingly hushed note, a national appeal has been launched for £250,000 to rescue Bath Spa from oblivion. It is from the report of the Bath Spa Trust responsible for this appeal that the commendatory sentences quoted in the last paragraph are taken. For the sake of the long-suffering British rheumatic public, this appeal must succeed, and it should obviously have a first call on the funds acquired as a result of the appeal of the British section of World Rheumatism Year which took place in 1977. If business sponsorship for the 1977 Bath Festival could be nearly doubled, then surely the even more deserving cause of Bath Spa should receive every support. The Department of Health and Social Security can apparently do nothing to help Bath Spa, but the Department of Energy can give £9000 to Bath University to investigate the constituents present in the hot springs which have served humanity all down the ages. Money, it would appear, can be found for Science and the Arts – but not for health.

This is a state of affairs which the public should no longer tolerate. If research is required into these hot springs, let it be into their healing virtues. Bath Spa must be revived to provide a valuable service to the rheumatic victims in our midst.

6

Cheltenham Spa

Cheltenham, in the midst of the Cotswold Hills, the 'Regency Town' as it calls itself, with a street, the Promenade, which *The Times* has described as 'perhaps the most beautiful thoroughfare in Britain', and '40 miles of avenues with some 40,000 trees', has never been able to make up its mind about its main claim to fame and tourist popularity. Spa, the Brighton of the Cotswolds, cultural centre, conference centre – all these it has been at different, and overlapping, times. Today it describes itself as having 'much to offer those who love a gay as well as a quiet life'.

As a spa its history dates back to 1716 (or 1715), when the Old Spring, on the site of which the Princess Hall of the Ladies' College now stands, attracted attention by virtue of the fact that it was frequented by flocks of pigeons. To the owner of the land, William Mason, this suggested some medicinal properties, a suspicion that was confirmed by analysis of the water, which revealed a high salt content. Much to the annoyance of the locals who were partaking freely of its water as a means of easing their rheumatics, Mason had it enclosed. He seems to have achieved little success, however, in exploiting its medicinal possibilities for the next we hear of it is around 1738 when Captain Henry Skillicorne appeared on the scene. A Manxman, who had made a fortune as a privateer (a perfectly respectable source of income for a sea-captain in those days), he retired to Bristol where he married a daughter of William Mason, who had also settled in Bristol. On Mason's death, Skillicorne moved to Cheltenham and settled on his late father-in-law's estate.

He immediately sensed the possibilities of the Old Spring, in spite of its derelict state, and decided to convert Cheltenham into a spa comparable to, if not better than, Bath. In this view he was encouraged by a laudatory reference, in a book entitled *History of Mineral Waters* published in 1740, to the Cheltenham Waters as the most effective in the country. He built a pump-room over the well and an assembly room and laid out tree-lined walks including the famous Well Walk. From these walks, it has been said, 'the present magnificent tree-lined Promenade has grown and Cheltenham's ordered terraces and squares of Regency houses have developed and are now acknowledged as some of the finest architecture of the period'.

The spa had its ups and downs in Skillicorne's time, having, for instance, only 450 to 650 visitors a year, according to his own diary, but what it lacked in quantity it apparently made up in quality, as among the visitors were Handel, Dr Johnson and Mr and Mrs Siddons.

Following his death in 1763 (incidentally his epitaph in St Mary's Parish Church, where he is buried, is said to be one of the longest in Britain) his sons had little more success, and it was not until around 1780, largely apparently under the influence of Dr Jenner of smallpox fame, who had a house in Cheltenham, that things began to look up for Cheltenham as a spa. This success seemed to be clinched when, in 1788, it was honoured by a visit from George III, accompanied by Queen Charlotte, with Fanny Burney as a maid-of-honour, and their three daughters. Progress, however, was still slow, but things began to move more rapidly when the Duke of Wellington decided that the waters of Cheltenham were good for his jaded liver, and not only paid several visits to the spa to imbibe them, but also strongly recommended them to his officers and their families. And, as every schoolboy knows, a recommendation from the Iron Duke was equivalent to an order from anyone else.

It was during the Duke's patronage that what the town proudly describes as 'the brightest jewel in its architectural crown' was conceived in the form of the Pittville Pump Room. This was 'the apple of the eye' of Joseph Pitt, lay rector of Cheltenham, banker and M.P. for Cricklade in Wiltshire, who had bought an estate on the north side of the town where wells had been dug and shown to contain medicinal waters. Pitt commissioned John Forbes, a local architect, to design a Pump Room which was to be the climax of the whole estate and named after him. The foundation stone was laid in 1825, and the building officially opened in 1830.

For some reason or other, as a Pump Room it was never a success, and the position was not helped by Pitt running into financial difficulties. Finally, to cut a long story short, in 1890 it was bought by the borough for the bargain price of £5400.

Anticlimax is the keynote of the next half-century, and the Pump Room's nadir was reached when it was occupied by United States and British troops during the Second World War, resulting

The Pittville Pump Room was designed by John Forbes and the foundation stone was laid on 4 May 1825. The building was completed in 1830 and the total cost was estimated at £90,000.

in a state of affairs graphically and tersely described in the admirably produced *The Pittville Pump Room Cheltenham*, published by the Borough Council. 'The ground floor of the Pump Room was used as an emergency food store, and the upper floors housed soldiers; generating stations were erected in the loggia, enormous Nissen huts fouled the greensward, and dry rot spread unchecked.' On derequisitioning, the Borough Council took up the challenge of restoration, and in 1960 the Pittville Pump Room was, appropriately, reopened by the 7th Duke of Wellington, and is now, according to the official brochure, 'available for hire for meetings, receptions, dinners, dances and similar private or public functions' – and, it might have added, the drinking, free of charge, of the waters which are pumped to a fountain in the main hall from a well 80 feet deep.

One unfortunate interlude falls to be added to this tale of the vexed history of the Pittville Pump Room. In July 1968 it was found that the well was polluted and, in the words of the official guide book, 'For the next three-and-a-half years Cheltenham went "dry", much to the fury of regulars and tourists alike. After much trouble, including the drilling of a new well, pure spring water was eventually discovered from an existing addit.' 'This means', it adds, 'that the water now available in Cheltenham is much the same as that handed by King George III to his Queen during their historic visit to Cheltenham in 1788.'

Analysis shows its major constituents to be (in milligrams per litre):

Calcium bicarbonate	150
Magnesium bicarbonate	229
Magnesium chloride	1945
Sodium bicarbonate	797
Sodium chloride	5430
Potassium chloride	15
Potassium nitrate	11

A good example of Cheltenham's ironwork in Priory Parade. *Cheltenham Borough Council:*

The Pittville water is also laid on at the Town Hall where a pump is replenished regularly from the Pittville Pump Room. According to Michael Rayward, the director of entertainments and tourism, who persuaded me to sample a plastic cup of it while he set an example by quaffing a cupful in the twinkling of an eye, there is a steady trickle, if not stream, of visitors to both sources to sample the water. He is toying with the idea of persuading some enterprising company to produce specially designed mini-bottles of it which visitors can take away as mementoes of 'a holiday in Cheltenham', thus recalling the days when it was bottled as the Cheltenham Natural Aperient Water.

On a more serious level the claim made by Cheltenham for its medicinal water is that 'Cheltenham Water is the only natural consumable alkaline water in Great Britain. The effect is mainly physiological, the chief action being antacid, mildly diuretic and laxative. The percentage of sulphates of magnesium and sodium, combined in the water with bicarbonate of soda, accounts for the unique properties of the Cheltenham Spa Water and to this is attributed its health-giving properties. "Taking the Waters", combined with a reasonably healthy way of living, pursuing especially a regime of moderation in all things, can contribute to a satisfying standard of physical health.'

Perhaps this is overstating the case – certainly in the absence of more precise evidence, the lack of which is a legitimate criticism of present-day research. In the absence of such evidence the scientifically orientated research worker who has such a stranglehold over medical research today, and is so vocal about it all, has no more right to criticise such a claim than the City Fathers of Cheltenham have to make it. The latter have at least the evidence of generations of visitors who claim to have benefited from a visit to Cheltenham including the drinking of the waters. And who are the research wallahs to deny such claims?

Perhaps the situation has been best summed up by that connoisseur of medical diplomacy, the eclectic 1st Lord Horder: 'Cheltenham is a centre for purveying the combination of health, rest, beauty and elegant entertainment – those inestimable things which people need more and more.'

7

Droitwich

Droitwich describes itself as 'a modest town which has developed quite independently of fashions and fads, but it has always been and still remains the salt of the earth of England'. Making allowance for the not unjustified pun, it is a fair description. Situated 6 miles from Worcester, 14 miles from Malvern and 20 miles from Stratford-upon-Avon, 'It offers', to quote the official guide again, 'a wonderful choice of country and places,' with a 'countryside rich in historical associations.' This compensates for the relative drabness of the town itself which, like Cheltenham, and to a lesser extent Bath, is tending to sacrifice its aesthetic aspects at the expense of attracting light industry as a source of income. From the point of view of its survival as a spa, which is the justification for including it in this review of British spas, it suffers from the disadvantage of being selected as one of the towns to receive the 'overspill' (horrid word) from the Birmingham conurbation, with a 'target' population of 30,000 (compared with the present 8000) by 1981, and inevitably the euphemistically described 'light industry' to provide employment for this influx.

Be all that as it may, it still deserves to be revived as one of Britain's spas that heal, its brine bath being unique in the United Kingdom, if not in Europe. Indeed, according to one modern writer on spas, 'For density and effectiveness there is no brine in the world to equal it.' One exception, however, must be made to this claim – the Dead Sea, which Israel, with an eye to the fullest exploitation of all its natural attributes, is developing on a large scale as a spa and health centre as recorded in chapter 15.

The ground upon which Droitwich stands, according to *The Spa in Medical Practice*, the revised edition of a report of a committee of the British Medical Association published in 1964, 'is rich in history'. Precisely the same words as are used by the 1970 official guide to the town. It is a history based upon salt, which was being exploited in pre-Roman days. But it was the Romans who firmly established the town as a salt centre, building a camp known as Salinae, the place of salt, in A.D. 45 to use to the full this rich source of salt, which they exported, not only to the rest of occupied Britain, but also to all the northern provinces of their empire. Incidentally, it is of interest that it is from the Roman custom of issuing a ration of salt to every soldier to salt down his winter ration of meat, and which was known as his *salarium*, or *salere*, that we owe the term 'salary' as used today. In due course the issue of salt, like that of rum to British sailors, was dropped and replaced by a cash payment, but the name, *salarium*, continued to be used for it, finally coming to mean the total remuneration of the individual.

From Roman days until 1922 the salt industry flourished in Droitwich. Indeed, it is to the industry that it owes its name. The original Saxon name was Wic, the origin of which is a matter of controversy, or at least mystery. Droit was added in Norman times, referring to the King's rights in the salt pits, which had existed since Saxon days. These were consolidated by a charter of 1215, whereby, in return for an annual rental of £100, King John granted to the men of Wic the rights of the salt pits 'to have and to hold from us and our heirs, to themselves and their heirs for ever, well and in peace, freely and quietly, peacefully and wholly honourably and fully'.

It was also around this period that Droitwich acquired its patron saint, St Richard. Richard de Burford, or Richard de la

Wych as he was later known, who was born in Droitwich around 1197, entered the Church where he had a brilliant career as a scholar and finally became Bishop of Chichester. One of the few occasions on which he revisited his native town coincided with the drying up of the Great Brine Pit, which faced the town with financial ruin. The Bishop was asked to bless it in the hope that this might restore the flow of brine. It did, and the town adopted him as its patron saint, dedicated the well, or pit, to him, and established an annual dressing of the well – whether in gratitude, or in order to prevent its drying up again is an open question that has never been solved.

Many centuries were to pass, however, before the commercially lucrative brine was to be used for medicinal purposes – and this was the result of a most curious incident. Precisely what happened is difficult to establish. There are at least three versions of the episode, agreeing in principle though differing in detail, but all are unanimous that it occurred during one of the cholera outbreaks of the 1830s. According to the official guide, 'A victim [of cholera] was ordered a hot bath, and to save time he was dipped in a vat of hot brine. He recovered, so that doctors repeated the treatment with other patients and with encouraging results.' This is the theme of all three counts, but the frills, if frills they are, in the other two variations are sufficiently interesting to make them worth reporting. One is that to cope with the epidemic of cholera, a hospital was extemporized from a disused salt-work. The medical orders were that each patient had to be given a nightly hot bath. One night, however, the bathman ran out of plain water, so he used buckets of hot brine instead, with most beneficial effects. The third variation is that the local doctors ordered frequent hot baths as a preventive. When the salt workers, who could afford neither doctor's fees nor hot baths, heard what their better-off compatriots were being prescribed, they solved the problem by jumping into the warm brine baths. The results of this were so impressive in warding off the disease that the wealthy were soon taking hot brine baths of their own.

Whichever be the true version, it was this episode that, for entirely the wrong reason, alerted the doctors of Droitwich to the medical possibilities of the local brine. They soon got their sightings right, however, and in 1836 the Royal Brine Baths were opened, and Droitwich was soon on the map as a spa for the treatment of the rheumatic and gouty aches and pains of mankind. The number of patients steadily increased, and some fifty years later, in 1887, the St Andrew's Brine Baths, the present establishment, were built.

For nigh on a century the St Andrew's Baths served Droitwich and its ailing visiting patients well, and earned world-wide renown for this ancient township. Latterly it was administered by the Droitwich Medical Trust, a charitable non-profit-making organization still in existence, governed by a council of management consisting of doctors and laymen interested in the restoration of health and in rehabilitation. As Tennyson reminded us, however, 'the old order changeth' and the bell began to toll for Droitwich spa in 1971, when the building was bought by the Droitwich Borough Council. In August of that year, 'to the regret of many thousands of rheumatic and arthritic sufferers' as a local scribe has justifiably put it, medical treatment at the Baths ceased, and the patients were transferred to the neighbouring Highfield Hospital for Rheumatic Diseases.

All, however, was not immediately lost. The large heated Brine Swim Pool, or Big Swim as it was known, was kept in being. Supervised by unqualified, but efficient and experienced, attendants, it was open seven days a week at a modest charge of 30p per 20-minute session, this time limit being set on medical recommendation. Under this regime, it is reported, 'Its patronage increased, many former patients using the pool as it is now the only brine available for easement of aches and pains.' In addition, it 'was used extensively by fit people for relaxation and pleasure and to ease tension.'

Meanwhile a working party was set up which recommended that this arrangement should be maintained while negotiations

St Andrew's Brine Baths, built in 1887. *Paul Mann.*

and planning were carried out for the use of the complex of buildings as an entity. In due course, recommendations were agreed in principle (always a forbidding clause) for a youth centre, sauna baths and treatment rooms, a large sports hall, a gymnasium and a restaurant, not to mention archery and squash courts. Special lifts and entrances were to be incorporated for the disabled. Hopes ran high that something might be salvaged from the characteristically maladroit action of the local authority, as is evidenced by the following excerpt from a brochure issued jointly by the Droitwich Borough Council and Droitwich Spa Association in December 1971. 'So it would seem that the new Droitwich will have a splendid health/sporting facility catering for enthusiasts of every age. Not only will the centre contribute to the expanding town population but regionally it will draw people together in a common good to seek and maintain physical fitness. Bearing in mind the steady progress made in all sectors Droitwich will indeed be a Spa town brought up to date.'

Alas, it was not to be. In January 1976 the following notice was issued by the Information Department of Droitwich Town Development: 'It is with regret that we have to announce the closure of the famous Brine Baths at Droitwich for economic reasons. Both the Wychavon District Council and the Droitwich Town Council are discussing the possibility of developing a new complex in the vicinity where it is hoped to incorporate warm brine bathing. However, it is not envisaged that the large Brine pool will be reopened in the foreseeable future.'

Such was the position when I visited Droitwich in the autumn of 1976. St Andrew's Brine Baths is an attractive building, nicely sited. Like all empty buildings it is somewhat eerie in its over-all effect on the visitor, the ghosts of its beneficial active past being far from laid. To revive it would be no difficult task provided those in authority – at the Elephant and Castle G.H.Q. of the National Health Service and in the hierarchy of the local regional hospital board – would take the requisite action. Equally essential is it that the regional medical fraternity should come off its high horse and pay some attention to the wishes of the local general practitioners and their patients. They it is, not to mention the thousands of patients from all over the British Isles – and overseas – who regularly visited this unique brine spa to benefit from its healing waters, who are in need of the help that Droitwich can supply. No other country in the world would neglect such a unique spa, and we might learn a lesson from Israel which is putting the comparable Dead Sea to such good use – not only therapeutically, but also to attract visitors, and their wealth, from all over the world.

The myopic approach of those in authority in closing the Droitwich brine baths is admirably and characteristically demonstrated by the fact that the water used to fill the therapeutic pool in the grandiloquently entitled Droitwich Centre for Rheumatic and Locomotor Disorders (*alias* Highfield Hospital) is ordinary water – not the brine water with all its healing properties. Here is a so-called centre for rheumatic disease sitting on top of a well-nigh unique source of natural waters of proven therapeutic value, yet it makes no use of them. My first reaction when I learned of this astounding fact was that perhaps it was a question of expense or some technical difficulty. But no; my investigations revealed that the therapeutic pool could have been connected quite easily to the brine water at little, if any, extra cost. To my possibly tactless, but persistent question, 'If not, why not?,' I finally got the reply that it was not done because of the pigheadedness of the local regional health authority. As an example of planning gone mad, no better example could be obtained.

Until 1971 the services provided by the St Andrew's Brine Baths covered the entire range of spa therapy, including deep pool therapy, reclining brine baths, aeration brine baths, brine douche spray baths, and brine mud baths, while electrical treatment and massage were also available as well as remedial exercises in a well-equipped gymnasium. This treatment, which was available to both private and National Health Service patients, was only given under medical direction. In addition, the Droitwich Brine Fund, established in 1937 by a generous benefactor, was available to provide financial assistance to those who required it if they were to benefit from Droitwich brine treatment.

The brine water is pumped up from a depth of 200 feet below the town, where it is believed to exist in the form of a lake formed by subterranean streams passing over beds of rock salt. No matter how much is drawn off, its water level never drops more than 8 inches. It is almost a saturated solution of sodium chloride, or common salt, being about ten times as strong as sea water, and with the same buoyancy as the Dead Sea. It reaches the surface at a temperature of 45° F. (7·2° C.), and is then heated to the re-required temperature. In the case of the large pool this was 93° F. (34° C.), a lower temperature than is customary in fresh-water pools. The reason for this is the stimulating effect the brine has on the skin.

It is this tremendous buoyancy bestowed by the high concentration of salt that gives Droitwich brine its unique therapeutic value. It enables patients to carry out movements which would not otherwise be possible or would be extremely painful. The floating position gives complete muscle relaxation whilst, because of the complete relief of body weight, patients can practise walking long before their legs are capable of bearing body weight on dry land.

All this has been admirably summed up as follows by an experienced physiotherapist.

> 'Patients are more manoeuvrable. This means that considerably more work can be got through during the time the patient is in the brine . . . The relaxation induced by the full support of the brine widens the range of pain-free movements in the many cases in which this is limited. Similarly, the degree of assisted movement which can be painlessly coaxed by using the assistance of buoyancy is surprising . . . The brine pool offers a medium for retraining which can be started early and continued longer to the benefit of the patient than is usual in ordinary water; even in quite late stages of the toughening of orthopaedic cases this factor assumes considerable importance, particularly where complete weight-bearing is not yet allowed. Because of the automatic supporting of the patients, the brine pool lends itself readily to class-working when patients can be grouped according to conditions. The amount of independence achieved by comparatively crippled patients during these classes is gratifying to them and to us, and, of course, the consequent economy of the physiotherapists' time due to such grouping is a big advantage.'

In other words, the Droitwich brine baths are ideal for the treatment of all forms of rheumatic disease, whether rheumatoid arthritis, osteoarthrosis, or generalized aches and pains, paralytic conditions such as poliomyelitis and strokes and other diseases of the nervous system such as multiple sclerosis, and the rehabilitation of patients involved in road, industrial and other accidents. In addition, the brine acts as a skin stimulant, which is valuable in treating the poor circulation which is a feature of conditions such as rheumatoid arthritis and paralytic conditions such as strokes and poliomyelitis. Incidentally, it is interesting in this context to note that one of the claims made for the waters of the Dead Sea is that they are of value in the treatment of psoriasis, one of the most troublesome and chronic of skin conditions. Finally, and never to be overlooked, is the psychological effect. To quote our physiotherapist again: 'Most patients thoroughly enjoy this treatment because it is a unique experience and because it is good fun.'

Yet this is the healing water of which the bureaucrats in the National Health Service – both lay and medical – have deprived our ailing citizens. And for no good reason. As in the case of every other British spa that has been closed down, the responsibility rests more on the rheumatologists, the specialists in this field, in our midst. Had they taken a strong line, it is doubtful whether the Ministry of Health would have closed the spas down. Droitwich is a particularly glaring example of blinkered specialists failing in their duty to the patients entrusted to their care. Apart from anything else, in the case of Droitwich there was an outburst of opposition from both patients and doctors when closure was first mooted. Thus, when I was in Droitwich I was shown a letter from one of our most distinguished physicians, a Fellow of the Royal Society, a knight, and a retired professor of medicine. He was badly crippled by arthritis of the hip and he had found that nothing gave him more relief than a course of treatment in the brine baths of Droitwich. In his letter he protested strongly against the closure of the baths. Yet no more attention was paid to his expert opinion than to the protests of all the many other patients who were to be deprived of a form of treatment that had done them so much good.

Droitwich, however, I am convinced, is still viable. The complex of buildings in which brine baths are housed may require some titivation, but this need not be unduly expensive. The subterranean source of healing waters is inexhaustible. The sooner it is re-harnessed to the service of suffering humanity, and the 'brine spa' of England is once again put on the map, the better. If ever there was a case for conservation of energy and natural resources, this is it.

8

Royal Leamington Spa

Royal Leamington Spa is the only surviving spa in the United Kingdom. Why it should have survived when equally viable ones such as Bath, Buxton and Harrogate have been allowed to fall into disuse is anyone's guess. The causes are probably multifactorial. They have certainly nothing to do with the constituents of its waters. They differ little in essentials from those in other spas. One factor may have been that it was one of the first to be municipalized and, whilst one holds no brief for local authorities as medical entrepreneurs, it may be that in this particular field the sobering influence of the municipality acted as an antidote to some of the more flamboyant social elements that made the popularity of other spas wax and wane, with corresponding financial strains on the owners of the spa establishments. Admittedly, following the granting of royal patronage, Leamington had its phase of fashionable popularity but this did not last for so very long, and the spa gradually settled down to a more sober middle-class existence, with visitors coming primarily for treatment.

In more recent times the reaction of the regional medical profession has probably paid a part. Certainly at the present day one of the reasons why it is still subsidized by the National Health Service is that few, if any, of the surrounding hospitals have facilities for hydrotherapy. Other forms of physiotherapy they can supply, but for hydrotherapy patients have to be sent to the Pump Room at Leamington.

Although at least one of the springs at Leamington – the saline one – had been patronized locally since the sixteenth century, it was not until 1784 that the history of Leamington as a spa really began. The *fons et origo* was the refusal of Lord Aylesford, the local landlord, to sell the well-site, which was on his property, to an enterprising Warwick doctor who had seen the financial possibilities in its waters. Lord Aylesford's laudable reason for repulsing the doctor's offer was that this would have entailed depriving the poor of access to the site.

This refusal stimulated William Abbotts, the landlord of a neighbouring inn, to search for a well on his own piece of land. Tradition lends a pleasing touch of drama to how Abbott's search at last achieved success. One day in 1784 (14 January, to be precise) he and a neighbour, Benjamin Satchwell, were standing on Abbott's piece of ground discussing the prospects in rather a despondent mood when Satchwell suddenly noticed bubbles rising to the surface of a pool in a neighbouring ditch. He immediately scooped some of the water up in his hands, tasted it and decided from its tang that it was the long-sought-for spring: an opinion that was confirmed on analysis of it by Dr Kerr of Northampton.

The sequel is admirably, if concisely, recounted in the 10th edition of *Where Shall We Go? A Guide to the Healthiest and Most Beautiful Watering Places in the British Isles*, one of a series of best-sellers issued by the publishers of this book in the latter part of last century.

> 'Very few of its visitors know how much Leamington is indebted for its present prosperity to the unwearied exertions of the shoemaker named Benjamin Satchwell. In 1784, this worthy man discovered a saline spring at "a little village of rude thatched clay cottages ranged round a dirty duck pond", called Leamington Priors, to distinguish it from

Regency buildings in Waterloo Place. *Warwick District Council.*

Leamington Hastings, another little village in the neighbourhood. He immediately endeavoured to draw attention to it; he went about talking of its capabilities, made appeals, wrote articles in the London papers and other places, and, at last, by his perseverance, managed to get the physicians to notice and recommend it – first Dr Kerr of Northampton, and then Dr Lamb, who wrote upon it. Then more springs were discovered. Sir Walter Scott published *Kenilworth*, which soon helped to bring fresh visitors to Leamington in order to visit the castle in the neighbourhood. Dr Jephson laboured indefatigably and successfully; and finally the Queen bestowed the distinction of "Royal" upon the Spa, which, as Princess Victoria, she had visited.'

Some of the details in this precise record of the coming to fame of this Royal Spa are worthy of note. In his pamphlet, published in 1794, Dr Lamb (or Lambe) forecast that Leamington was 'likely to cast Bath and every other Spa into the shade'. What finally put it on the map was the patronage of royalty, first of the Prince Regent, a frequent visitor to Warwick Castle, and then of Queen Victoria herself. This brought the aristocracy, those who aped them, the local landed gentry, the rich and the famous, including the Duke of Wellington, Longfellow, Dickens and Ruskin, who greeted the 'cure' the water had produced in him with the intriguing comment: 'My health is in my own hands. I have gone back to brown potatoes and cherry pie.' The Dr Jephson mentioned was a local doctor who played a leading part in establishing the spa. For some reason or other he was not approved of by Ruskin, who referred to him as a quack. His fellow-citizens, however, had no doubt about the value of his services, and he is commemorated by the beautifully laid out Jephson Gardens on land presented to the town in 1843 by Squire Willis, and by the housing of his statue in a pleasing Corinthian tower.

The town itself, built on the banks of the somewhat sluggish Leam, variously called the 'queen of Inland Watering Places' and

The Jephson Memorial. Dr Jephson was a local doctor who played a leading part in establishing Leamington as a spa. *Warwick District Council.*

the 'Garden Town of Shakespeareland', has been more soberly described as 'a flourishing and well-balanced community of over 40,000 persons'. As an example of town planning and landscape gardening it may not quite compare with Bath or Cheltenham, but it still retains in its centre some of the elegance of the gracious days of the Regency and early Victorian era. Situated in the heart of England – an ancient tree is said to mark the centre of the country – it is cheek by jowl with Warwick and Kenilworth, and not too distant from Stratford-upon-Avon. A modern conference centre, opened in 1972 by the late Lord Avon, is its latest effort to attract visitors.

The Royal Pump Room is situated in the heart of the town, facing the Jephson Gardens and backing on the Royal Pump Room Gardens, which between them occupy 21 acres. The first Pump Room and Baths on the site were built in 1814. They paid handsomely in their early days, but by 1848 the fashion of taking the water had begun to decline, and in 1860 they were threatened with closure. This so shook the local inhabitants that a new company was formed to take over the building. Extensive reconstruction was undertaken and they entered on a new sphere of activity, which still persists to the present day when, in the words of an official hand-out, 'The Council with the advice and cooperation of its Medical Advisory Committee, and encouraged by the National Health Service, has carried out many developments.'

The spa waters, which are inexhaustible, are natural saline waters of the muriated sulphate variety. Their source is the saliferous marls which form part of the lower Keuper beds and red sandstone, upon which the town is built. The origin of the springs is attributed to a primeval sea which once covered the rock strata underlying the town. Analysis shows the following constitution (in parts per million):

Sodium	345·12
Potassium	1·56
Magnesium	24·56
Calcium	68·01
Iron	0·05
Chloride	580·00
Bicarbonate	7·08
Silicate	0·24
Sulphate	181·90

They thus closely resemble those of Homburg, Kissengen and Wiesbaden. Whilst today the major interest in the use of the waters is hydrotherapy, there is a tap in the Pump Room, and one outside the building, where the spring waters can be drunk, and I saw both being used during the course of my visit in the autumn of 1976.

As a prelude to an account of the present-day activities of the Pump Room, a further extract may be given from *Where Shall We Go?*

'The mineral waters of Leamington may properly be divided into three classes: saline, sulphureous, and chalybeate, "containing in various proportions oxygen, azote, and carbonic gases; the sulphureous springs containing also sulphuretted hydrogen, with sulphate of soda, the chlorides of sodium, calcium and magnesia, and in some instances silica, peroxide of iron, and traces of iodine and bromine." This water is used both internally for drinking and externally for bathing. In drinking, four to six weeks are necessary to give the waters a fair trial, and a much longer period to derive the full benefit of their virtues. The average quantity taken is a pint, which ought to be drunk first thing in the morning, by sipping it slowly, half before walking, and the rest after brisk exercise, and always at the spring. If taken in undue quantities, it is apt to irritate and injure the bowels. If the sulphureous water produce headache and sickness, or unduly excite the excretions, the patient is not (in all probability) receiving benefit from it. The chalybeate is valuable as a tonic and diffusible stimulus for persons of weak, lax, and pale habits of body, and is regarded as favourable in cachexia.'

The Pump Room, now under the management of the Warwick District Council, is well equipped. This includes quite a large hydrotherapy pool filled with warmed diluted saline spring water. All treatment is individual, with one aide per patient under the general supervision of a physiotherapist. In addition, a full range of physiotherapy is available, and there is also a small gymnasium. I was also interested to learn that they use a lot of hot packs – made from fuller's earth bought from a branch of a well-known multiple chemist.

During the course of a year some 50,000 to 60,000 treatments are given to around 5,000 patients, for which a sum of about £160,000 is received from the Department of Health and Social Security. This sum is based on a proportion of the running costs of the whole complex. National Health Service patients are only treated on the recommendation of consultants from neighbouring hospitals. The area covered in this way by the Pump Room covers practically the whole of the Warwickshire Health Area, including Rugby, Stafford, Coventry, Stratford and Warwick. Many of these hospitals have their own physiotherapy department but none of them do hydrotherapy.

Many of the patients come by ambulance, an excellent shuttle service being provided by the Area Authority. Only on relatively rare occasions does the system break down, as on the day I visited the Pump Room when a major motorway pile-up occupied the services of all available ambulances. In such emergencies, naturally, spa treatment comes low on the scale of precedence. Private patients are also treated on the recommendation of their general practitioners, but there have been relatively few of them since the last war. There is no medical officer attached to the Pump Room, treatment being prescribed by the referring consultant, but not a few of these, wisely, leave the details of treatment to the senior physiotherapist.

The Pump Room complex also includes a sunny rest-room where patients can relax after their treatment and, if they so wish, drink the spring saline waters. To complete the complex there is a quite impressive and most attractively decorated Pump Room Restaurant, open to the public, where morning coffee, lunch and afternoon teas are provided to the accompaniment of commendably muted background music of not too modern origin. It can also be hired for evening parties. The Corporation does its own catering, and, if the morning coffee I had is anything to go by, maintains a high standard.

Such then is Royal Leamington Spa – the only British spa that has been spared to maintain a great tradition. I was impressed by what I saw of it, its staff and how it is run. Perhaps it could do with a little titivating here and there, but it compared favourably with some of the continental spas I have seen. It is a living argument in favour of spa therapy, and one can only hope that, not only will it be allowed to maintain its service to those who can benefit from it, but that other area and regional health authorities will follow its example. Where there is scope for its development, which might also be a help in financing it, is in attracting private patients from home and overseas. In these days when tourism is such a lucrative source of foreign currency, the potentialities of Leamington should be exploited to the full. On the question of to what extent the facilities of the Pump Room could be extended, I found local expert opinion divided. Certainly more staff would be needed, but this should involve no real trouble. The doubtful point is how many more patients could be treated in the available space, even with additional staff.

That, however, is a minor point. The main thing is that Royal Leamington Spa should be allowed to continue its good work as a spa that heals – efficiently, safely and congenially.

9

Buxton

For some reason or other Buxton has never received the popular acclaim to which it is entitled. Although situated roughly midway between Manchester and Sheffield, each around 25 to 30 miles distant, neither city has really patronized it, though it is by no means neglected by trippers, daily or otherwise, who, in the quaint Edwardian language of a 1904 guide book, 'The sunshine brings out like daisies and daffodils.' As the unofficial capital of the High Peak District, it has historical, architectural and scenic, as well as medical, claims to distinction. Situated at a height of around 1000 feet, it is said to be the highest town in the United Kingdom, one of the five golf courses in its neighbourhood claims to be the highest in England, and the nearby well-known hostelry, The Cat and Fiddle Inn, at a height of 1690 feet, is the highest inn in England.

This geographical trilogy of height records has the drawback, of course, of a climate that, to quote our 1904 author again, 'is indeed apt to prove trying . . . Bracing its friends call it, but its enemies might say bleak . . . One should never go to Buxton without being prepared for chilling experiences even at the height of the summer.' 'But', he generously admits, 'if one does have the luck to fall in there with a spell of fine weather, nowhere can it be more enjoyable than among upland Derbyshire's rich store of varied natural beauties.' A somewhat more tolerant attitude is that of that delightful period piece, *Where Shall We Go?*, according to which the climate of Buxton in the summer is 'more attractive than Bath, which is hot and comparatively oppressive, besides being so thoroughly "town", while Buxton is entirely "country" . . . On the whole it is bracing and healthful.' Obviously, even by the turn of the century a degree of Edwardian decadence was beginning to dilute the Victorian hey-day of back-to-Nature. Actually, recent figures show a mean annual temperature of around 46° F. (8° C.) with an annual average of around 1050 hours of sunshine (6 hours a day during May, June and July), and an annual average rainfall of around 51 inches (130 cm). The comparable figures (in round numbers) for Bath are a mean annual temperature of 50° F. (10° C.), an annual average of 1530 hours of sunshine, and an annual average rainfall of 31 inches (79 cm). But perhaps it is symptomatic of Buxtonians' appreciation of the importance of the weather to their flow of visitors that the town's Meterological Station is situated somewhat ostentatiously on the top of the Slopes, the piece of parkland facing the Crescent.

In the Domesday Book it appears as Baukestanes, which is conjectured to be derived from one of the rocking-stones still found in other parts of the area. But its modern version comes from Buckstone, which dates from the days when north-western Peakland was a Royal forest, and the King's deer overran the Wye valley, in which the town lies, congregating for shelter in the Buxton basin and drinking at the warm springs. These were the thermal springs which had led the Romans, a thousand years earlier, to establish the settlement known as Aquae Arnemetiae (The Spa of the Goddess of the Grove), complete with baths, remains of which have been found at different times, but never preserved.

What happened after the Roman exitus is unrecorded, but by the Middle Ages the thermal springs were being regularly patronized by the locals for their healing power, and by the twelfth century a chapel had been erected nearby, dedicated to St Ann (sometimes spelt Anne), variously described as the patron saint of cripples, and of sacred, or healing, wells. The walls of the chapel were hung with the crutches of those who had sampled the waters, been cured of their crippledom and had gone on their way rejoicing, leaving their crutches behind as evidence of the miracle that Mother Church had achieved. This evidence of Popery was more than the reformers could tolerate at the time of the Reformation, and in 1538 the chapel was closed and the well blocked up by order of Henry VIII.

Apparently, however, you can no more keep a good well closed than you can keep a good man down, and within a matter of half a century the well was not only reopened but drawing such crowds that the Poor Law of 1572 contained a special clause that provided that, 'Whereas a greate number of pore and dyseased people do resorte to the Cytye of Bathe . . . and the Towne of Buckston . . . for some Ease and Reliefe of their Diseases at the Bathes there, and by means thereof the Inhabitauntes of the same Cytye of Bathe and Toune of Buckstone are greatly overcharged', hereafter 'no dyseased or ympotent poore person living on Almes' shall be permitted to visit either place unless he has received a licence from two Justices of the Peace and is provided for by the place from which he comes.

It was not only the hoi polloi who were flocking to Buxton to benefit from its healing waters, and it is at this stage that the Earl of Shrewsbury, with his wife, the famous Bess of Hardwick who married him as her fourth husband, appears on the scene as the progenitor of Buxton as a modern spa. As the local laird he built Buxton Hall, adjoining St Ann's Well, for the accommodation of those who came to the well, and provided nearby lodgings for destitute visitors. The Earl's main claim to fame is as the gaoler of Mary, Queen of Scots, who in 1573 was given permission to visit Buxton to sample the waters for her health. While in Buxton she lived in Buxton Hall. She made subsequent visits, the last in 1584, when she is said to have inscribed the following lines on a window pane at the Hall:

> *Buxtona, quae calidae celebraris nomine Lymphae*
> *Forte mihi post hac adeunda Vale!*

which has been translated as:

> Buxton, whose fame thy milk-warm waters tell,
> Whom I, perhaps, no more shall see, Farewell!

A fitting regal, if pathetic, farewell. She was executed three years later.

By this time Buxton was being recognized as a spa of considerable social standing, its patrons including the Earl of Leicester and Lord Burghley, but it was a century later that it really came to the fore and the first signs began to appear of what one can recognize as the Buxton of today. For this development the credit goes to the Cavendish family, into whose hands the town and its surroundings had fallen through Bess of Hardwick. She had persuaded one of her husbands, Sir William Cavendish, to establish himself in Derbyshire, where they built the original Chatsworth and became the owners of Buxton. Their son was created Earl of Devonshire in 1618, and the third Earl's son was created Duke of Devonshire.

It was the fifth Duke who decided to put Buxton on the map as a spa comparable to Bath and Cheltenham. The times were in his favour. 'The growing use of stage coaches', as it has been put, had 'resulted in the conversion of the hitherto almost impassable driftways and pack horse trails of England into roads,' with the result that travelling had become safer and more widespread. What had hitherto kept Buxton back was its inaccessibility and its lack of comfortable accommodation for visitors. This state of affairs the fifth Duke (there is only one Duke in Buxton; further specification is unnecessary) set about rectifying in what can only be described as a grand style. A former habitué of Bath, he had been impressed by what the Woods, father and son, had done there architecturally, particularly with the Circus, completed in 1765, and the Royal Crescent completed in 1775. As a classical scholar of some repute, and a grandson of Lord Burlington, the authority on the Palladian style of architecture, he decided to build a Palladian crescent in Buxton, and for this purpose commissioned a Yorkshireman, John Carr, then the leading Palladian architect in the country.

The Crescent, as it was, and is, known, was completed in 1784 and, as has been rightly said, 'Buxton is indeed fortunate to be known by its Crescent, a stately pillared stone building in the form of a segment of a circle with an arcade running the whole length of the segment. This structure is of three storeys, built in the Doric order of architecture.' John Carr, justifiably, looked upon it as his masterpiece. Originally it was occupied by three hotels as well as some private lodging houses, and to provide stabling for the guests the Duke had built at the back of it, on what is now the site of the Devonshire Royal Hospital, a magnificent stables – the Great Stables – housing 110 horses, and with accommodation for grooms and stable boys, as well as a large half-acre central exercise court capable of holding 300 horses. Again John Carr was the architect.

It was from these Great Stables of all places that sprang the Devonshire Royal Hospital. The story dates back to the days of Elizabeth I, when such was the influx of the 'invalid poor' that a charitable fund, the 'Treasury of the Bath', was set up to help them. From the time of the earliest extant records (the report for 1785) of this Bath Charity, as it came to be known, following apparently an ancient precedent, funds were collected by means of a levy on visitors, hotel and lodging-house keepers having collecting books and each visitor being expected to subscribe not more than a shilling. The scope of the Bath Charity is shown by the fact that between 1820 and 1858 nearly 4000 patients benefited from it. By this time it was felt that a hospital was required to house those patients and in 1854, under the presidency of Edward Bulwer Lytton, an appeal was launched to build a hospital.

From this stemmed, in 1858, the presentation to the trustees by the sixth Duke of half of the Grand Stables, and these premises, duly adapted, were opened as the Devonshire Hospital in 1869.

A poster advertising Buxton, dated May 1857.

Over the next twenty years the seventh Duke presented the rest of the Stables to the hospital and the whole ensemble was completed in 1881 by a gift of £24,000 from the Cotton Districts Convalescent Fund. This included the covering of the half-acre former exercising yard by a dome, which has the distinction of being the largest single-span dome in Europe with a diameter of 164 feet – greater than that of St Peter's, Rome.

This must be the most magnificent physiotherapy department in the world. Certainly I have never seen anything so impressive. Around it, and opening on to it, are consulting rooms, wards, treatment rooms, occupational therapy rooms and the like, while patients do their controlled exercises in the hall itself, and underneath it are the baths, supplied with spa water. To stand in the centre of the hall and look up at the glass dome and the gallery that runs round it, where other offices are housed, is an experience I shall never forget. It is impressive without being overwhelming, grandiloquent yet still homely, attractive yet still utilitarian. For some reason one does not feel lost in its immensity. Appropriately, on one wall of the hall is a series of photographs of each of the sixth to eleventh (the present) Dukes.

The Crescent also included a magnificent Assembly Room decorated in the style of Robert Adam, which for long was the centre of social activity. Alas, as so often is the case, it fell on evil days, becoming a privately run clinic and finally a geriatric annexe to the Devonshire Royal Hospital. When this was transferred to a new unit the Assembly Room remained empty for four years and was only saved by commendable enterprise on the part of the County Council, Buxton Corporation, the Department of the Environment and the Department of Health and Social Security, following its purchase by the Derbyshire County Council in 1970 as an area library. At a cost of £150,000 it has been completely renovated, including its magnificently painted roof, the design of which was still clearly visible, and the repainting of which was done with authentic colours and gilding. The mahogany doors with their original handles, inlaid with mother of pearl, were refurbished, and the original crystal chandeliers, which were still in position, were taken down, washed and polished, and rehung. In addition, wall lights, which would probably have been in position originally, were specially designed to match the chandeliers.

Situated on the first floor, and approached by a quite impressive circular staircase, it is a superbly proportioned room, and must be the most beautiful public reference library in the country. The only reservation one had on viewing it was that it was unfortunate that it could not be used for its original purpose. But perhaps the day may not be too far distant when, having regained some of its old glory and popularity as a spa, Buxton Assembly Room will become the social centre of the High Peak.

Across the road from the Crescent, and nestling at the foot of what was known as St Ann's Cliff and is now named The Slopes, is the Pump Room which was built in 1894. Now the Information Centre, it houses St Ann's Well where the water can be sampled (at a price) either neat or diluted with orange juice. It can also be bought in bottles (20p for a large, 700 millilitre, bottle; 10p for a small bottle). As under the old Inclosure Act the waters of the Well must be available to the public free of charge, the Corporation had to erect a free pump just outside the Pump Room. Both these sources are much used, as I gathered when I visited Buxton. Not only do people come to the free pump, which is the legal St Ann's Well, to drink a cup or glass of the water, they arrive by car and fill up carboys or plastic containers of it to take home.

Indeed, so popular is it that it threatens to become big business. For many years a local bottling company has bottled it, the water being pumped through silver-lined lead pipes to the factory, which is situated just behind the Crescent. How big the sales are no-one seemed to be quite certain, but the High Peak Borough Council is said to make £1700 a year from selling it in the Pump Room. Plans are now afoot for the local bottling company, with one of the biggest producers of mineral waters in the country, to launch out on a campaign to sell Buxton Water in a big way. This new development has been stimulated by the current interest in spa waters, presumably due to the large number of people who nowadays indulge in continental holidays. There they learn to drink such traditional waters as Vichy, Contrexéville and Evian, and the never-failing French entrepreneurs are now pushing their specialities over here in supermarkets and elsewhere. The natural reaction to this on the part of Buxton and the British bottlers is, why leave this unmet market to the French when we can provide equally effective spa waters in this country? So great is the interest in Buxton Water, I was informed, that, if the current negotiations should break down, there are several other firms, including a continental one, which have asked to be put on the list as potential bottlers and vendors of the blue waters of Buxton.

The characteristics of the Buxton water are that it is warm, has a comparatively high gaseous content, mainly nitrogen with some carbon dioxide, argon and helium, and has calcium as the predominant mineral constituent. It issues from the ground at a temperature of 82° F. (28° C.), and there is a daily flow of 200,000 gallons (2 million litres). The water when seen in depth has a beautifully clear blue colour with bubbles of gas constantly rising to the surface: this, when the sun shines on it, gives an incredibly attractive iridescent appearance and fully justifies the description of Buxton as the 'Spa of the Blue Waters'. Opinions differ as to its taste – some dislike it, others like it, but it certainly could not be described as unpleasant. What, however, the fathers of spa therapy would have thought of the present owners of the Pump Room offering the option of drinking it with orange juice is another matter.

At the moment it is pumped to three different places: the Devonshire Royal Hospital, the public swimming pool opened by Princess Anne in 1972, and the Buxton Bottling Company. This, together with what is drunk in the Pump Room and at St Ann's Well, represents only a fraction of the daily flow. The rest, literally as well as metaphorically, goes down the drain. Incidentally, I was interested to learn in Buxton that, under current legislation, spas must have permission from the local water authority to use spa water and, if such permission is given, have to pay for the privilege. Thus at the moment Buxton is paying £500 a year to the local water board for the use of the 200,000 gallons a day that its wells produce. A nice tax on health!

What of the future of Buxton as a spa? Of all the spas I visited its prospects are the brightest. Indeed it is providing the full range of spa therapy, though, for some reason, this is not being publicized. At the Devonshire Royal Hospital, with over 200 beds, a full range of such treatment is being given, including what is officially described as hydrotherapy – but this hydrotherapy includes the use of the spa waters. In other words, the local National Health Service hospital is providing its patients, both inpatients and outpatients, with more or less the full range of spa therapy, while patients can supplement this, if they so wish, by drinking the waters in the Pump Room or at St Ann's Well.

What I could not discover was whether private patients could obtain treatment at the Devonshire Royal Hospital. If not, there seems to be no reason why they should not do so as outpatients, which is what most of them would require. In this respect Buxton has the unique attraction of its superb domed physiotherapy department which would compensate for any lack of the privacy that some private patients might desire. Should it not be possible for the Devonshire Royal Hospital to cope with an influx of private patients, there are two sets of baths owned by the Corporation, one at either end of the Crescent, known, respectively, as the Natural Mineral Water Baths and the Thermal Baths. The former are on the site of the original Roman baths and the present building, which was closed in 1966, was entirely rebuilt by the Corporation and reopened by the then President of the Royal College of Physicians of London in 1924.

No-one seemed to be quite clear why there should have been two separate sets of baths, or how they got their names, as they both used the same water. One suggestion is that the so-called Thermal Baths were the more exclusive socially and were used for private patients, while the others were used for what used to be known as panel patients. I was not able to see the Thermal Baths, but I did see over the Natural Mineral Water Baths. They are certainly suffering from the inevitable decay of disuse, but should be quite capable of being put into operation again.

As with everywhere I went, those responsible for running Buxton had been so indoctrinated by the rheumatologists as to the uselessness of spa therapy that they were in a complete quandary about what to do with these two sets of baths on their hands. Obviously they cannot be allowed to lie derelict for an indefinite period of time, but it is sincerely to be hoped that it will be possible to restore them to their original use before they are converted into bingo halls or the like. On the other hand, there is no reason why one should not be converted into a casino, when the law permits, and the proceeds used to re-equip and subsidize the other as a spa treatment centre. Alternatively, if £150,000 could be found to restore the Assembly Room – a most commendable example of conservation – surely £250,000, say, can be found to restore one or both of these baths to their original laudable use.

On the social side Buxton has also much in its favour. It has an opera house which seats 600 to 800. This was built in 1903 and the ceiling paintings were executed by Italian craftsmen. At the moment it is used as a cinema but could easily revert to its original purpose, though the backstage arrangements would require a fair amount of money to bring them up to modern standards. On the other hand, judging from the comments one hears about the backstage equipment in many provincial theatres being used regularly, this should be no insuperable obstacle to the Buxton Opera House being put back to its original use. Why not, for example, a 'Glyndebourne' Summer Season done by the Welsh Opera Company? With Manchester and Sheffield within easy access, such a season would almost certainly be a popular success, especially as you can walk direct from the Opera House into the Pavilion, owned by the Corporation, which has full restaurant facilities and overlooks the beautifully-kept Pavilion Gardens.

The Pavilion also incorporates a concert hall, which can, and has, housed the Hallé Orchestra. Built in 1876, it is a most impressive cast and wrought iron building, with excellent acoustics, which is being used increasingly as a conference centre. Next to it is a small Playhouse Theatre. The Pavilion complex – for complex it is, built in cast and wrought iron throughout and aptly described as 'a Victorian pier not over the sea but over a park' – ends in the swimming baths I have already mentioned. All in all therefore Buxton has the facilities for providing a full range of social activities.

To this must be added its scenic attractions. It is a natural centre for the High Peak District which contains some of the finest scenery in England, and within easy access are some of the best-known buildings in the country, such as Chatsworth House,

The Crescent, designed by John Carr of York, and built between 1780–4. *From an engraving after E. Dayes, 1803.*

Haddon Hall, Hardwick Hall and Keddleston Hall, which claims to be 'probably the finest Robert Adam house in England'.

In every way Buxton therefore has reason to be optimistic about its future, not only as a tourist centre but also as a spa. The essentiality of the spa element for its successful development is stressed by Mr Gordon Cullen, the architect and town designer, in his recent report on the town commissioned by the British Tourist Board and published in *Resorts and Spas in Britain*. His ideas may be somewhat flamboyant by medical standards, but they are none the worse for that, and medically they are basically sound, stressing as they do the importance of the social side of spa life in the renovation of the visitor and his restoration to health. Buxton is already a spa that heals. All that is needed is initiative, both lay and medical, to extend these facilities and make them more attractive, and more available, to a wider public.

10

Harrogate

Harrogate has sold its spa heritage for a mess of pottage, and with a smugness that is somewhat surprising in hard-headed Yorkshiremen. That is always assuming that there is such a distinct genus of the human race. The more people I meet in different parts of the country, the more sceptical do I become of these much-vaunted but entirely unproven regional differences. Whether they be Yorkshiremen, Lancastrians, Mancunians, Liverpudlians, Geordies or Cockneys, they are fundamentally the same, the only differentiation, as often as not, being their accents. We are such a conglomeration of racial genes – Picts, Celts, Romans, Saxons, Vikings, Normans and Huguenots – that it is impossible to sort us out into neat categories. In any case, human nature is basically the same, no matter where it originates, susceptible to all sorts of factors, such as environment, as well as genes, so that prognostication as to how a child will develop is just as hazardous and unreliable as forecasting the economic future of a country. How many a 'hard-headed' Yorkshireman, for instance, who has made good by his shrewdness and the sweat of his brow, has been succeeded by a ne'er-do-well son who has squandered his father's hard-earned fortune?

Be all that as it may, the story of Harrogate as a spa is not one of which the town has any reason to be proud. The attitude of the

City Fathers is perhaps nowhere better summed up than in the preface written by the Town Clerk to *An Atlas of Harrogate*, published by the Corporation in 1963: 'I think it can be said that Harrogate is one of the few places to which the 1939–45 War was a blessing in disguise.' His reason for this curiously commercial outlook on a holocaust such as the Second World War is that, 'Whereas prior to this all the eggs were in the "spa" basket, the town's economy is now based on five principal foundations and has never been sounder than it is today.' Of these 'foundations', its spa activities come second last: 'It is still a spa and holiday resort with as many treatments being done, in conjunction with the Leeds Regional Hospital Board, as during its hey-day as a spa.' Seven years later, in 1970, so far as the Corporation was concerned, it was as dead as a dodo in respect of its spa activities, to which it owed its origin. Indeed, such a scunner did the Harrogate powers-that-be take to their heritage that, according to 'one council man', as reported by the *Guardian* in 1977, 'Harrogate doesn't like to be thought of as a spa at all.' A classical example, surely, of the offspring of a self-made successful business man trying to disguise his origins.

The history of Harrogate as a spa dates back some four hundred years, when it was a mere collection of straggling houses ensconced in the Royal Hunting Forest of Knaresborough. Adjoining it was a spring. Whether or not it had any special significance among the locals is an open question which will be discussed later, but it owes its significance as the foundation of modern Harrogate to Captain William Slingsby, the enterprising seventh son of the local laird. Coming upon this spring one day he was impressed by its similarity in taste to the waters of Spa, in Belgium, which he had sampled in the course of his travels. At least that is the explanation given by Dr Edmund Deane, a York doctor, in his *Spadacrene Anglica or The English Spaw Fountaine* published in 1626, in which he records that the gallant captain, 'drinking of this water found it in all things to agree with those at the Spaw [i.e., Spa in Belgium].'

Another version of the story, however, is that what attracted Slingsby's attention was its 'ruddily stained banks', which, of course, were due to the fact that these were iron-containing, or chalybeate, waters. This is not the only mystery, or controversy, surrounding Tewit Well, as it came to be known. Practically all the books on the subject, including Dr Deane's, refer to Captain Slingsby having made his discovery of the medicinal value of the well in 1571. As has been pointed out, however, if this were so, he must have been a child prodigy as he was born in 1562, and would have been only 9 years old. A more likely date is 'about the year 1620', as suggested in Camden's *Britannia*. His connexion with the neighbourhood is certainly definitely established in 1597 when, through his father's influence, he became Member of Parliament for Knaresborough.

The spring became known as the Tewit Well from the peewits which frequented it, and Slingsby had it protected with a wall. It was given pride of place in two books published in 1626: that of Dr Deane already mentioned, and Michael Stanhope's *Newes out of Yorkshire*, both based on visits paid to it the previous year. They found it neglected and choked with dirt, but were able to clean it up and sample the water. According to Deane, it purged the blood of 'cholericke, phlegmaticke, and melancholic humours. It cheereth and reviveth the spirits, strengtheneth the stomacke, causeth a good and quicke appetite, and furthereth digestion.' In 1631, Stanhope discovered a neighbouring chalybeate well, which became known as St John's Well.

Much more important, however, to Harrogate's future as a spa were the sulphur wells. Although Deane and Stanhope gave priority to the Tewit Well, they both discussed the sulphur waters and noted, with distaste, that these were used both for bathing and drinking by the 'vulgar sort', particularly for skin diseases. Thus, according to Stanhope, what became known as the Old Sulphur Well was 'open for the promiscuous use of all sorts . . . so that the poore Lazar [i.e., leprous] impotent people do dayly environ it, whose putrid rags lie scattered up and downe, and it is to be doubted whether they do not wash their soares and cleanse their besmeared clouts (though unseene) where diverse after dippe their cups to drinke.'

How long these sulphur wells had been used in this way is not known. It is known that there were several holy wells in the area, dating back to the Middle Ages if not to the days of St Mungo (seventh century), that were popularly endowed with specific medicinal properties. And, as has been said, 'It is therefore not improbable that a well which advertised itself by "a most unsufferable Suphurie fume, at the first not easie to be endured", should have been well known locally for a long period before the arrival of the first inquisitive outsiders.'

It was not, however, until after the Restoration that Harrogate began to assert itself as a spa in its own right, hitherto having been known as Knaresborough Spa. The first inn in High Harrogate, the Queen's Head, was opened in 1687, followed by two others, the Dragon and the Granby, before 1700. By 1756, according to *The Life and Opinions of John Buncle, Esq.*, 'With the greatest civility, cheerfulness and good humour, there is a certain rural plainness and freedom mixed, which are vastly pleasing,' while in 1763 Dr Alexander Carlyle, the famous Scottish divine, was singing its praises, noting that it was much frequented, not only by Scots, but also by the English nobility and gentry. He mentions that while he was there, staying at the Dragon, Lord Clive was in residence at the Granby. An interesting social distinction existed as late as 1839, when Dr A. B. Granville, in his three-volume *The Spas of England, and Principal Sea-Bathing Places*, published in 1841, recounted that, 'The Dragon and the Granby were sacred places. The Lords only graced the latter, while the wealthy commoner pleased himself in the former.'

A somewhat different picture was presented by Tobias Smollett in his masterpiece, *The Expedition of Humphrey Clinker*, published in 1771, when he has Matthew Bramble saying: 'Harrogate is a wild common, bare and bleak, without tree or shrub, or the least signs of cultivation; and the people who come to drink the water are crowded together in paltry inns, where the few tolerable rooms are monopolized by the friends and favourites of the house, and all the rest of the lodgers are obliged to put up with dirty holes, where there is neither space, air, or convenience.' His description of the bathing routine is even more devastating. On the other hand, he painted a brighter picture through the lips of Jeremy Melford: 'At present, the company is more agreeable than one would expect from an accidental assemblage of persons who are utter strangers to each other. There seems to be a general disposition among us to maintain good fellowship, and promote the purpose of humanity, in favour of those who come hither on the score of health.'

The 'wild common' to which Matthew Bramble refers is in actual fact one of the saving features of Harrogate which prevented it from falling deeper into the hands of scheming builders, such as George Dawson who, for example, in the 1880s sold to the Corporation for £29,500 an estate he had bought four years earlier for £19,500, knowing that the Corporation was interested in it. Smollett's 'wild common' is what is known as the Stray. An area of 200 acres, it was initially part of the Royal Hunting Forest of Knaresborough, over which common grazing rights were enjoyed. By the 1770 Enclosure Act it was preserved for all time as an unenclosed 'stinted' pasture in order that, 'All persons whomsoever shall and may have access at all times to the said springs [Tewit and St John's], and be at liberty to use and drink the waters there arising and may have use, and enjoy full and free, ingress, egress, and regression, upon, and over the said two hundred acres of land.'

As has been noted, it 'gives the town so much of its character', though on a dull, rain-threatening day, such as when I saw it, it can be quite bleak. It is hemmed in today on all sides by houses, some representing the quintessence of English domestic architecture at its worst, and is crossed by several busy roads (the Harrogate motorist has no respect for pedestrians) and the railway (fortunately in a cutting). The two wells it contains are both in a disgraceful state, particularly St John's Well, and neither provides any water – so that the 1770 Act is not being complied with in so far as 'all persons whomsoever' are not 'at liberty to use and drink the waters there arising'. There is a tap outside the pump-room built over St John's Well in 1842, but it is not working, and I was interested to read in *A History of The Wells and Springs of Harrogate* by Bernard Jennings, published by the Corporation in 1974, that, 'A free outside tap for the supply of the chalybeate water is temporarily out of service.' It was still in this state in 1977 – but then perhaps Yorkshiremen's sense of time may be different from that of other people.

Equal neglect of its spa heritage is shown in the other open space that gives Harrogate its character – the Valley Gardens, or Bogs Field as it used to be known until the Corporation decided

The Montpellier Baths, built in 1835 and demolished about 1890. *From a chromolithograph by W. Monkhouse.*

that a more genteel name was required. But, before dealing with these 'world-famous' gardens, as the official guide-book describes them, the history of Harrogate as a spa can be brought up to date.

It was in the 1840s, after the coming into force of the Harrogate Improvement Act 1841 (which created Improvement Commissioners) that things began to move. This involved a changing emphasis from High to Low Harrogate. High Harrogate, at a height of around 600 feet, was the origin of the town as a spa, as it was here that the Tewit and St John's Wells were sited. In time, however, the importance of the sulphur wells, which were in Low Harrogate, at a height of around 350 feet, began to predominate. Today they constitute one township, but for long High Harrogate looked down on Low Harrogate, socially and commercially as well as physically. Visitors, however, gradually became tired of the relatively long trek from their hotel in High Harrogate to the Pump Room and baths in Low Harrogate, and by the turn of the present century what had formerly been Low Harrogate had become the spa centre with all the major hotels distributed round it. Two other factors came into play. One was the arrival of the railway in 1848; the other was the increased wealth brought by the industrial revolution, giving rise to a new clientele for the spa of the *nouveau riche* of the West Riding.

In 1868, in the words of the Corporation's historian, 'The Improvement Commissioners began a programme of expansion which by the end of the century brought the whole of the spa area of Low Harrogate under municipal ownership [Harrogate was incorporated as a borough in 1884], and furnished it with unequalled facilities amongst British spas.' This involved, amongst other things, the population increasing between 1851 and 1911 by 916 per cent. In 1897 the Royal Baths, in which were gradually concentrated all the bathing facilities, was completed at a cost of £118,000. In time this replaced all the other treatment centres, with the exception of the Royal Pump Room, which had been built in 1842, and was used entirely for the drinking of the waters. Some idea of the extent of the work done is given by the figures for August 1898, when 52,851 glasses of spa water were drunk and 18,723 baths were given. Throughout the Victorian era the tradition of early-morning drinking of the waters was retained, and in one single morning in August 1901, 1800 visitors were served with the waters at the Royal Pump Room between 7 and 9 am – and this was by no means exceptional. So great indeed became the congestion that an annexe (solemnly opened by the Lord Mayor of London) was added in 1913.

In 1886, the Corporation bought Bogs Field, with its thirty-five wells within an area of 170 by 40 yards, and opened it as public gardens (Valley Gardens). The wells here are a mixture of sulphur and chalybeate, and as we have seen, had been known at least since the seventeenth century. In the eighteenth century a sulphur and a chalybeate spring were assigned for the use of the poor, and when the Bath Hospital (now the Royal Bath Hospital) opened in 1826 it tapped three of the springs. In due course the bulk of the waters was pumped to other treatment centres, but one pump-room, known as the Magnesia Well and containing a mild sulphur water with magnesia, was installed in the Gardens. This still exists, with a tap outside from which the public are supposed to be able to draw off water for drinking – just as there is a tap outside the old Royal Pump Room, which is now used as a museum – but neither of these, like the Tewit and St John's taps, is functioning. The Corporation is apparently determined that even the odour of sulphur waters should not be allowed to contaminate the modern conference atmosphere of what they grandiloquently describe as 'The Floral Resort of England'.

In the early Victorian era Harrogate was still predominantly a north country spa, with its clientele largely drawn from the local squirearchy, supplemented later, as already noted, by the *nouveau riche* of the 'dark Satanic mills' of the West Riding. During the nineteenth century this regionalization widened and by 1910, more than one visitor in eight came from London. This was, according to one observer, at least partly because it was, 'A particularly useful place to stay between the end of the London season and the beginning of grouse shooting from Scottish country seats.' It was never patronized, however, by royalty to any great extent, though its historian proudly recalls that, 'On an August day in 1911, there were no less than three queens in the Spa, Queen Alexandra, Empress Marie of Russia and Queen Amelie of Portugal,' adding the cryptic note: 'These were far from the only royal visitors that particular year.' Edward VII and his sister-in-law, the Tzarina of Russia, were among those who, in the words of one observer of the social scene, 'helped to give the town an aura of somewhat ponderous regality'.

In this context of Russian royalty, one of my most interesting experiences was the discovery at the north end of the Stray, beside one of those murderous roads traversing it, of a neglected-looking stone cross. The superscription was so eroded as to be almost indecipherable, but I ultimately made it out. The cross was to the Glory of God and was erected by the Grand Duchess George of Russia as a memorial to nine of her patients who had been killed in the First World War. The Grand Duchess lived in Harrogate for many years and established Heatherdene and two other hospitals. It was to these hospitals that these nine men had been admitted as war casualties and had recovered sufficiently to return to active service and make the supreme sacrifice. On a dull, sunless, bleak day there was something particularly moving about this isolated and neglected memorial with its tribute from a member of a sadly stricken royal family to a small group of men whom she had been responsible for nursing back to health – only to join the ranks of the glorious dead who died that we might live – and I stood in bowed silence for a moment of time.

The rest of the story can be briefly summarized. Harrogate as a spa survived the First World War as shown by the following number of treatments given at the Royal Baths:

1901	96,000
1927	120,207
1936	76,665
1938	89,174

These included the Chancellor of the Exchequer and the Postmaster General in 1932.

Writing in 1919, a medical observer described Harrogate as, 'probably the most popular and best patronized of all British spas', adding that, 'Probably no resort possesses a greater number of highly qualified physicians, there being something like one to every 500 of the population.' An almost infinite variety of treatments was provided: at one time, it is claimed, 'More than forty different types of mineral baths were available.' These included brine baths, the brine being obtained at one time from Middlesbrough. Peat baths were incorporated in the regime, and thereby hangs a tale of Yorkshire caution. For long the peat was bought from Piestany, the Czechoslovak spa famous for its peat baths. Whether Piestany started raising its price, or whether a canny Yorkshireman kicked at paying the price demanded, I know not, but investigations were initiated into finding a local source. This was soon tracked down to the nearby moors, in the form of peaty earth charged with organic acids and containing a small proportion of iron. According to a contemporary account the process of preparation was as follows. 'The peat is first cut, broken up and mixed in a mechanical mixer to the consistence of a thick pulp; it is then placed in the bath and raised to the required temperature by live steam, which is driven through it.' 'These operations', it is noted, 'take place outside the bathroom; when ready, the bath is run on rails through an aperture in the wall into the bathroom proper, where there is a second bath of plain-water to be taken after the peat for purposes of cleanliness.' So all was well, the local 'peat' served the purpose, both doctors and patients were satisfied and costs cut considerably.

So great was the run on the Royal Baths that they had to be extended. The extension, completed in 1939, may soon have seemed a white elephant when visitors were replaced by evacuated Government employees during the Second World War, but this was not to be the case. The introduction of the National Health Service saw a steady rise in the number of treatments given until they exceeded the pre-1939 total, rising to more than 150,000 in some years. These were practically all National Health Service patients from the areas of the Leeds and the Newcastle Regional Hospital Boards. Only around 9 per cent were private patients. So bright was the prospect that, writing in 1963, the historian of the Corporation reported that, 'Harrogate as a spa is still very much alive.'

Alas, his prognostication was delusionary. In 1969 the Royal Baths closed so far as the National Health Service was concerned. A gallant attempt was made to keep them going, an official brochure announcing that, 'The Royal Baths of Harrogate have been reorganized after the termination of their National Health Service contract, and in future only private patients will be treated.' The experiment ran for a year but received so little support that it was terminated. And so ended a glorious era of enterprise, stretching back nigh on four hundred years.

Seven years later, when I visited the town, it was clear that the Corporation had moved heaven and earth to remove all the evidence it could of the town having been a great spa. 'Conference Centre' is the new catchword, and no money is being spared to attract conferences, trade fairs, exhibitions and the like. The official guide book grandiloquently claims that, 'Situated at the centre of Great Britain, Harrogate makes an ideal venue for conferences, trade fairs and exhibitions,' with an 'Exhibition Complex' (*pace* the psychiatrists) including the Royal Hall with accommodation for 1350. This is the building which was erected at a cost of £70,000 and opened by Sir Hubert Parry in 1903. Built in the hey-day of Harrogate as a spa competing hard with, and emulating, the great German spas, it was known as the kursall, but rapidly changed its name in 1914 to the Royal Hall.

Not satisfied with this current 'complex', 'The Council of the Borough of Harrogate', we are informed, 'are at present heavily involved in planning further extensions to the Exhibition Centre.' In another of its leaflets it has what can only be described as the impertinence to say that, 'Harrogate's legacy', from its great days as a spa, 'is the antique shops and fashion houses, displays and exhibitions, hotels and fine architecture.' I know nothing of antique shops or fashion houses, but 'fine architecture' it certainly does not possess. Its architecture is not bad, but it shows a complete lack of initiative and planning, and the town is not a patch, as schoolboys used to say, on Bath, Cheltenham or Buxton. Nor has it the rural charm of Strathpeffer.

The only remnant – and it is literally a remnant – of the spa era is that there are Turkish and sauna baths in the Royal Baths. These I visited, and was impressed by the remaining parts of the old baths in which they are housed: nicely wood-panelled changing rooms, and one bath still left and in use – with the classical tiling so beloved of the Victorians. I was shown over by the head hydrotherapist who had many regrets over the 'good old days' when the baths were dealing with thousands of patients rather than hundreds, though it is interesting that in this pathetic hangover of one of the most magnificent and best-equipped spa treatment centres in the country – equal to anything on the Continent – they still have 300 to 400 patients (or clients) a week.

The only other part of the old building the Corporation has done anything to preserve is the old Assembly Room. As this was occupied by some trade exhibition of plastic furnishings, I could not see it properly. But, in spite of the ghastly exhibits, it proved quite an attractive room, though not comparable to its opposite number in Bath or Buxton. It has, however, been repainted, and with reasonable taste, and undoubtedly makes a pleasant restaurant and occasional exhibition centre.

Carefully preserved – whether with mature forethought, a delayed feeling of remorse at what had been lost, or quite accidentally, I know not – it is a fitting epitaph of the great days when Harrogate was a spa that healed, with the following superscription that stretches round its four walls:

> Ah! What avail the largest gifts of Heaven when drooping health and spirits go amiss. How tasteless then whatever can

be given. Health is the vital principle of bliss and exercise of health. Then in life's goblet freely press the leaves that give it bitterness; nor prize the healing waters less, for in the darkness new light and strength they give.

And over the entrance is inscribed the prayer:

Benedicte Fontes Domino. (Bless the fountains, Oh Lord.)

Elsewhere, as I have already indicated, the Corporation has done little, if anything, to preserve its historical spa monuments, a state of affairs that can only be described as a national scandal in these days of conservation of our national heritage. None of the three outside sources of the spa drinking waters is functioning. The two historical original springs on the Stray – the Tewit and St John's Wells – are in a state of neglect, particularly the latter, and nothing has been done to commemorate or even mark the site of the many springs in the Valley Gardens that have been closed. The only attempt to preserve the past is the use of the Royal Pump Room, which closed down as such in 1939, as a Spa Museum. This is quite interesting but could definitely be improved, including making it easier for visitors to see the Old Sulphur Well, as it was known, over which it is built. This can be arranged on payment of a sum of money, but visits are certainly not encouraged. The least that could be done would be to open it up, make it easy of access and allow visitors to drink the waters (at a price) if they so desired.

Incidentally, while on the subject of drinking the waters, I was interested to learn on my visit that Harrogate was following the example of Buxton and was seriously considering the idea of bottling one of the more benign of its milder spa waters on a commercial scale. At the moment mini-bottles are sold as a gimmick in the Information Centre, the bottling being done in a nearby hotel. So far as I could make out, no attempt was being made to restart the sale of Harrogate Salt as it was practised in the seventeenth century, when the inhabitants spent part of the off-season boiling large volumes of sulphur water to extract Harrogate Salts which were sold as far afield as London.

In view of the criticism of spa doctors of the past by their successors today that they produced no research work to support the claims they made for spa waters, it is interesting that a higher proportion of such research came out of Harrogate than almost any other spa. Much of this was provided by Dr William Bain, who practised in Harrogate for many years, and whose son, happily still with us and for long on the staff of the Harrogate General Hospital, became one of the leading cardiologists in the country. Dr William Bain wrote two books on the subject. The first one, written jointly, on *The Physiology and Therapeutics of the Harrogate Waters, Baths and Climate Applied to the Treatment of Chronic Disease*, was published in 1905; the second, on *The Pharmacological Action of The Harrogate Drinking Waters*, came out in 1935. In these, as in many other articles, published in such leading journals as the *Journal of Physiology*, he reported much valuable work on the efficacy of the Harrogate waters, and it is interesting that in his second book he criticised the Corporation for having been 'very remiss not to have made some attempt to ascertain the value of its assets' – i.e., its spa waters. He ends with an appeal to the authorities, 'to carry out a detailed examination of the seventy-odd springs with the object of finding some additional therapeutic agents and thus adding to the medical resources of Harrogate'; adding, 'It would further tend to place the spa treatment of disease upon a more rational and scientific basis.'

That this appeal should have fallen on deaf ears – both municipal and medical – is the tragedy of this modern township of 64,000 inhabitants with its eighty-eight mineral springs producing an almost unique range of natural waters: strong and mild saline sulphur; alkaline sulphur; saline iron; and alum. With a first-class hospital (the Royal Bath Hospital) of 160 beds, and an energetic department of rheumatology in the neighbouring Leeds University, it is in an excellent position to become one of the leading spas in the United Kingdom, if not in Europe. It is better served with hotels than any other spa town in the country, and as a holiday centre it has within easy reach a range of ancient abbeys and cathedrals second to none in this or any other country. With its easy accessibility, and a climate that is no more unreliable than that of most other tourist centres in this island home of ours, it has everything that a spa needs for success.

To suggest that this resurrection of its spa activities would clutter the town up with the old and decrepit is a figment of the pathological imagination of its misguided councillors. The modern spa is of value to all ages, and not only to those who have been crippled by the ravages of age and disease. It is to the middle-aged, threatened with incipient rheumatic afflictions, that the facilities of a spa appeal, especially if these can be associated, as they are in Harrogate, with other forms of relaxation to make a stay there not only a healing process physically, but also a relaxing process emotionally and mentally. Inevitably, there will be a certain proportion of the crippled and the disabled, but they are no blot on any township and indeed must be looked upon by any charitable country as a section of the community deserving of all the help that can be given them, and no self-respecting member of the community is going to be put off by their presence.

Let Harrogate therefore reopen its spa facilities and thereby restore to the ailing citizens of this country the right to make full use of its eighty-eight mineral springs which give it the right to call itself a unique spa that heals, and emblazon on its coat of arms the prayer over its Assembly Room:

Benedicte Fontes Domino

11

Woodhall Spa

Woodhall Spa owes its existence as a spa, quite incidentally, to a member of a well-to-do Lincolnshire family who went bankrupt in an attempt to find coal. It was in 1811 that John Parkinson decided that a field next the manor of Woodhall was the place to look for coal. At not inconsiderable expense, therefore, he had a shaft sunk for this purpose. At a depth of just over 500 feet the shaft was suddenly flooded with a rush of water. Work had to be suspended while, with considerable difficulty, this stream was diverted. In due course this was accomplished and operations for sinking the shaft were resumed – but to no avail so far as coal was concerned.

Parkinson, however, seems to have been a born optimist – or a confirmed speculator (the terms are often synonymous) – and continued spending his decreasing wherewithal in sinking his shaft to ever greater depths. In this misbegotten optimism he was, unbeknown to himself, supported by the subterfuges of his miners. At least, tradition has it that, 'Mindful of their continued employment, they took down pieces of coal in their pockets to bring up again, convincing their master that untold riches were only inches away.' 'Such discoveries', it is recorded, 'caused considerable excitement; Parkinson was besieged with would-be investors and once the bells of nearby Horncastle were rung to proclaim the discovery of coal.' Finally, at a depth of around 1000 feet, Parkinson went bankrupt, all further work was suspended, and the mouth of the derelict shaft was planked over.

The water, however, continued to gush and in due course reached the surface, overflowing into a neighbouring brook. In course of time the water was drunk by some of the locals who immediately realized that it was not ordinary water. Inevitably this suggested to the countryman's mind that it might have some healing virtues, and in time stories of its miraculous properties began to circulate. Some said it cured rheumatism – the bane of the Fenman's life; others said that it revived sick animals.

This was the state of affairs when Thomas Hotchkin, the Lord of the Manor, acquired the property and, when he found that it relieved his gout, he decided to do something about it and to cash in on this unexpected discovery. He therefore built a pump-room and a bath house over the well and, as there were no houses in the neighbourhood, what a contemporary writer nicely described as, 'a neat and unostentatious edifice which serves as an hotel honoured with the name of Victoria Hotel'. This was completed in 1839.

Considering the primitive means of communications in those days, the news of the healing properties of this new medicinal well must have spread rapidly. In *The Spas of England*, published in 1841, Dr A. B. Granville wrote that, 'Though recently discovered the Spa has not lacked visitors. On examining the register kept at the pump-room, I found from twenty to thirty inscribed in each day in the month of August. In the space of seven weeks from the end of May, 970 had taken baths . . . and altogether in the course of the twelvemonth, about 2000 had bathed. Those who drank were only 300.' To this he adds an interesting sociological note: 'Judging from the names, I should imagine that the majority of the visitors were farmers and people belonging to the industrious classes. Indeed, neither the bath-room accommodation nor the pump-room are calculated for very superior classes or persons.'

Gradually, however, its fame spread throughout the land. For some years access was difficult but, after the railway reached Lincoln in 1848 and Woodhall seven years later, Woodhall Spa was firmly on the map, and visitors became ever more numerous. Much of this success was due to a Dr Cuffe to whom the baths and hotel were leased from 1862 to 1883, and who acted as resident medical superintendent. Among his many innovations was a small cottage hospital for poor patients in 1873. Up to 1884, however, Woodhall Spa consisted merely of the Spa Baths and the Victoria Hotel, standing in their extensive grounds of around 100 acres, some half-dozen houses, and St Andrew's Church built in 1846.

Expansion was obviously not only necessary, but likely to be lucrative, and in 1887 the Spa property was sold by the Hotchkin family to a local syndicate which reconstructed the Baths and the hotel and added, as it has been put, 'every available apparatus for utilizing the mineral water', while the hotel's 60 acres of grounds provided 'delightful sheltered walks and recreation lawns'. In the words of Dr Lionel Calthrop, a one-time medical superintendent of the Spa, 'This fresh enterprise led to such an increased annual influx of visitors that there speedily grew up by the side of the Spa and grounds a prettily laid out town with hotels, residential villas, boarding houses, shops, sports club, and all that a modern health resort requires for the accommodation and recreation of its visitors.' This included, incidentally, an 18-hole championship golf course, laid out originally to the plans of J. H. Taylor and Harry Vardon, and variously described as, 'one of the finest inland courses to be found anywhere in Great Britain', and 'one of the top three courses in the country'. Other more essential, if more prosaic, developments were the Alexandra Hospital, with 30 beds, for those who could not afford to pay for private treatment, and the Tor o' Moor Home for Gentlewomen of Moderate Means.

Unfortunately, nemesis overtook the Victoria Hotel. In 1920 it was burnt to the ground, never to be rebuilt as it had not been

The Pump Room, Woodhall Spa, in 1888.

sufficiently covered by insurance, and the company which owned it could not afford to replace it. Indeed, the fates have not been kind to the hotels of Woodhall Spa. The Royal Hotel, built around 1895 as a rival to the Victoria Hotel, and the owner of which sank his own well so that he could provide spa water for his exclusive use, was destroyed by a land-mine in the Second World War.

Woodhall Spa successfully survived the First World War and, after a somewhat seamy background experience at the hands of speculators, the spa establishment centre was offered free of charge by Sir Archibald and Lady Weigall, who had purchased it, to the local Urban District Council. Their generous offer, however, was declined on the ground that there was no by-law authorizing them to expend money on such a venture, in spite of the fact that in previous years they had subsidized the 'Baths' to the extent of a penny rate for 'ablution' purposes. To overcome this bureaucratic bumbledom a Charity Trust was established – the Woodhall Spa Baths Trust – to take over the establishment. And such is the position today.

During the Second World War the baths were commandeered as an ablution centre for the thousands of R.A.F. personnel encamped in and around Woodhall Spa. After the end of the War the Spa centre, not as badly mutilated as most buildings are after military occupation – as for example at Cheltenham (see chapter 6) – was restored to its original use. On the introduction of the National Health Service in 1948, the Sheffield Regional Hospital Board took over the Alexandra Hospital, but declined to take over the Spa establishment from the Trust. An arrangement was therefore come to whereby the Board agreed to use the establishment and pay *pro rata* for treatment given there to National Health Service patients. This is the arrangement still in force, except that instead of a *pro rata* payment, the National Health Service pays a lump sum covering running costs, including salaries of staff, and apparatus, while the Trust pays for upkeep and maintenance of the buildings and any capital expenditure.

This plan seems to work well. Not the least of its advantages is that it gives the Trust and the staff room for expansion and improvement. Typical of this is the new hydrotherapy pool that the Trust was able to build a few years ago. As was pointed out to me, this would not have been built yet if it had had to take its place in the National Health Service waiting list of 'planned projects'. Instead, being convinced that it was necessary, the Trust was able to go ahead and have it built. As a result of this, and other improvements, Woodhall Spa proudly claims to be 'the most up-to-date hydrotherapy centre in the Eastern Counties'. That it is no more is regrettable, but that is a point that can best be discussed after a review of Woodhall Spa today.

The town – or township – with a population of around 2500, lies midway between Boston and Lincoln, 'almost exactly in the centre of Lincolnshire' according to one authority. (Incidentally, it is interesting – or perhaps the psychologists have some subtle explanation for it – how spas have a habit of claiming to be at the centre. Thus, Leamington is at the centre of England, while Harrogate is at the centre of Great Britain.) At one time with a direct train service to London, taking $2\frac{1}{2}$ to 3 hours, it must now be one of the most isolated towns in the country, having experienced one of the most searing of the notorious Beeching cuts. The nearest railway stations are Boston and Lincoln, each 20 miles away, and the bus service is about as scanty as it could be. Sampling public transport, it took me over four hours to get there from London by two trains and one bus. If this is how British Rail treats an attractive health resort, it is not surprising that the British Tourist Authority is finding it so difficult to develop the tourist attractions of the country to the full.

It is a most attractive spot – far removed from the traditional picture of the dreary damp Fen country. Actually it has one of the lowest rainfall averages in the country and claims to 'enjoy the driest climate of all the British spas'. In addition, it has a high sunshine record. Its climatic advantages are due to a combination of factors. It has a deep, sandy gravel sub-soil so that the ground dries rapidly, and there is a minimum of ground mist or miasma. It is sheltered from the north and east by the 500-foot high Lincolnshire Wolds. Above all it is thickly wooded, which not only provides protection from the wind but also adds a charm that is lacking in any of the other spas I visited. The Spa Centre itself is situated in woodland surroundings which bring a sense of peace and calmness which is unique in spa circles, with the exception of Strathpeffer. As one guide book expresses it: 'With its modest Pump Room, tree-lined roads and sylvan setting, the spa appears remarkably rural when compared with such sophisticated healing-centres as Bath and Cheltenham.' It is this that gives it what another guide book describes as its 'unusualness', amplifying this by noting that, 'The spacious woods and gardens of the Spa are in the centre of the town; even the golf-links [lovely Scottish phrase!] are only five minutes' walk from the post office.' While most of the woods are pine or beech, there is one of oak known as the Waterloo Wood, as it was raised from acorns planted immediately after the Battle of Waterloo.

Granted that the sun was shining from a nearly cloudless sky when I visited it but, even making allowance for this, the over-all impression was one of an ideal site for a spa. Not the least of its attractions is that the general standard of domestic architecture, apart from an occasional patch of dreary depressing late-Victorian and Edwardian housing, is commendably high. Even the most modern houses, of which there are quite a few (all, incidentally, well planned and laid out with neat, well-kept, reasonably-sized gardens) were very attractive on the whole. When I inquired how this pleasingly high standard was maintained, I was told that it was because an increasing number of professional, Service and business men are coming to the town for their retirement. Equally impressive was the absence of 'light industry', that fungoid growth that is ruining spas such as Cheltenham, Llandrindod Wells and Droitwich. This is rural England at its best, relatively unspoilt by the hand of man.

The surrounding countryside, though attractive, may not be rich archaeologically or historically, though Somersby, Tennyson's birthplace, is only 11 miles away, and, of course, the superb Lincoln Cathedral and the unique St Botolph's Church (the Boston Stump) are only some 20 miles away. The champion golf course has already been mentioned, and in addition there is excellent trout and coarse fishing. But, perhaps equally important in a spa, the flat countryside with its ample sylvan footpaths provides the ideal surroundings for those who, either by preference or by force of circumstances, wish to obtain their exercise by ambling through the countryside, especially as this is literally available at their doorstep without having to brave the roar of modern traffic.

So far as the Spa is concerned, the unique feature of its waters is their high content of iodine and bromine. There are one or two Continental spas which possess either iodine or bromine waters,

The Pump Room, Woodhall Spa, in the mid-1930s.

but in none of them is the content as high as the Woodhall waters, and in none of them is this particular combination to be found. In addition, they have a relatively high salt content, which means that they are ideal for bathing in as the high salt content makes it much easier to move the limbs. In this respect they are in no way comparable to the waters of Droitwich, but the resulting increase in specific gravity is sufficient to make this aspect of their use of real value. The fact that the salinity is not particularly high means that the waters can be drunk, which, of course, cannot be said of the Droitwich waters.

As already mentioned, the waters at one time were used for both drinking and bathing purposes. Hence the original pump room where the waters could be obtained and drunk. The recommended time for drinking was before breakfast, the action being mildly purgative, and anything up to a pint was consumed at a time. It has a definitely salty taste. So popular were the waters at one time that they were bottled and, according to one advertisement, 'can be obtained through any Chemist in the United Kingdom or direct from the Secretary, Woodhall Spa Co. Ltd.' at a price of 1*s.* 3*d.* per bottle. The prescribing of drinking of the waters at the Spa itself was abandoned in 1930.

The Woodhall Spa Rheumatism Clinic, to give it its modern plebeian, if descriptive, title, is housed in the old Spa Baths and Pump Room, or Victoria Baths as it used to be known. As already mentioned, this is beautifully sited in woodland surroundings, though only a few minutes' walk from the centre of the town. Peace and quietness is the keynote, and perhaps it was appropriate that I heard my first cuckoo of the year as I approached the building. It is, of course, not very old – the Spa itself is little over a hundred years old – but parts of the original building still exist, though this has been considerably modified and added to in the course of the years.

Today the main entrance, which was the one used by private patients (the 'hoi polloi' were admitted by a back entrance to a different part of the building where they received their treatment without mixing with the 'elite'), takes you into the pump room. This has a lovely stained pine roof, and facing you as you enter is the small orchestra gallery which was in use throughout the day, providing music for those partaking of the waters. Unlike many other spas, where the waters were dispensed from a fountain or from a central 'bar', here the waters were obtained from two taps at the far end of the room. Today the taps have gone and the orchestra gallery has been walled in, but otherwise the room is relatively unchanged, being used as a reception room and waiting room. A current adaptation, which pleased me, is that the walls are hung with pictures painted by local artists. These are on sale, the Trust collecting a small commission on each sale. A quick glance suggested that the standard was commendably high.

The rest of the 'clinic' provides the full range of physiotherapy, including the new hydrotherapy pool which has already been mentioned. Unfortunately this is filled with ordinary water, and not the mineral water from the original well over which the clinic is built and which can still be seen. The official reason given for this is that the well water became contaminated and could not be sterilized. Hence the use of chlorinated tap water. This did not strike me as an altogether convincing reason for giving up the use of water which, apart from any other merits it might have – and, as in every spa I visited, these have never been scientifically investigated – has a sufficiently high specific gravity to facilitate the increased use of crippled, deformed or rheumatic limbs.

There was, however, another reason, and that was the rapid corrosion of metal pipes induced by the well water when heated to the temperature necessary for use in the pool. This, it was claimed, involved considerable expense in the way of replacing the pipes. Incidentally, no new problem, but one which previous generations had faced up to. The alternative was to use plastic piping, which would not be corroded, but the installation of such piping would be difficult and expensive. I was assured that this problem of corrosion had been referred to the experts, who had concluded that there was no way of counteracting it. The final argument against using the well water was the interesting one that the corrosion would also affect the hoist used to facilitate the immersion of badly crippled patients in the pool. As the experts had reported that such corrosion was inevitable and unavoidable, it was not possible to obtain insurance cover against any resulting harm to patients. A superb argument in these litigious days.

I have gone into this story in some detail to illustrate the difficulties one is up against in trying to save our spas that heal. When I was young I was taught that difficulties were created to be overcome. Today they are used as an excuse for taking the line of least resistance. And in this particular instance it is the patient who suffers.

The clinic is open all the year round, and the number of attendances runs around 17,000 a year. These are dealt with by a staff of two whole-time and three part-time physiotherapists with the assistance of several aides. The patients, practically all of whom are National Health Service patients, are drawn from the whole of Lincolnshire, and are brought to the clinic by an ambulance shuttle service. All patients are seen by the consultant in rheumatology and rehabilitation for the area, either at the clinic or in the various hospitals in the county which he visits regularly. He is also responsible for patients in the local Alexandra Hospital. These are all inpatients and are brought to the clinic for treatment by a local car service. There are practically no private patients nowadays – perhaps ten a year. These are mostly patients referred by local general practitioners and are seen after the usual clinic hours.

An interesting historic echo is that mud packs are no longer used in spite of the fact that this used to be one of the routine forms of therapy. The 'Woodhall Spa Mud or Fango', as it was known, was described as 'the pure rock from which the mineral water is derived'. This was obtained when the well was emptied for cleaning purposes every decade or so, and apparently sufficient 'mud' was obtained in this way to meet the demand until the next cleaning. In addition, the supply was supplemented by the sediment from the two large tanks into which the well water was pumped prior to use in the baths. In those days there was no communal pool, merely individual baths. In the words of Dr Lionel Calthrop, 'It contains all the bromo-iodine and saline constituents of the water and forms a very effective medium for the carrying out of the fango or mud treatment by means of packs.' 'It is applied', he explains, 'to joints and limbs and other parts of the body as required and a course of this form of treatment for arthritis and neuritis has proved very beneficial.' An interesting alternative to such mud packs was what was known as motherlye. This was prepared from the mineral water by evaporating it over steam coils until it was condensed into saturated solution. According to Dr Calthrop, this was 'much used in the making of compresses for applications to painful joints, and for adding to douches and sprays where a strong local reaction is desirable, and is often very effective in joint disease'.

Such then is the sad tale of Woodhall Spa. Unlike Droitwich, Harrogate, Llandrindod Wells and Strathpeffer, its premises are still in use, but its unique waters have been discarded – and without any attempt to prove, or disprove, the claims that have been made for them over a span of a hundred years. This is a state of affairs for which there is no justification. The approach is the negation of all sound scientific principles. Here is a unique opportunity to investigate the effect on the human body, in health and in disease, of waters, the like of which exist nowhere else in the world. They have been condemned without trial on what can only be described as grounds of prejudice.

As is emphasized again and again throughout this book, hydrotherapy is not synonymous with spa therapy. It is an essential part, indeed *the* essential part, of spa therapy, but only if the local waters be used – at least until the opponents of such spa waters produce convincing scientific and clinical evidence that they have no advantage over ordinary water. Why should literally millions of pounds be spent on producing new, often dangerous, drugs for the treatment of rheumatic conditions, and an almost unlimited amount of time and skilled man-power on testing these on scientific principles, when neither State nor doctors are prepared to give an iota of attention to these healing waters so liberally provided by Nature?

Further, spa therapy takes care of the whole man – not merely his aching and deformed limbs, joints and muscles. This psychological aspect of spa therapy is scoffed at by the brash young rheumatologist, but as he grows older he will realize that it is an essential component of the treatment of disease. When I visited Woodhall Spa I was told of the Lincolnshire farm labourer with osteoarthrosis of the hip – a common affliction of the farming community in the Fens – who contended that he only kept going because of the two to three weeks he spent in the Alexandra Hospital every year. It was this alone that kept his rheumatics under control – and it was not merely the treatment that counted; just as important was the rest and relaxation he obtained away from his daily routine.

This, I was assured, was by no means a unique case. And the same principle applies throughout the whole social spectrum: housewives, professional and business men alike. To get away from the kitchen sink, the office, the desk, the factory, and to be able to relax in a comfortable hotel in pleasing surroundings while receiving skilled therapy from experts who are sympathetic and understanding – such is the ideal. Such is the treatment that was offered by British spas for many years, and is still offered by Continental spas.

It is in providing such over-all comprehensive care that Woodhall Spa has so much to offer. And the sooner it is restored to its former glory, and the medical profession allows the local authority and hoteliers to attract those patients who will benefit from its many attractions, including its mineral waters, the better. This is medicine as it should be practised – and must be practised – if the nation's massive expenditure on health is to be justified.

12

Welsh spas

Like the Highlands and Islands of Scotland, Wales has a long tradition of healing, or holy, wells, dating back to before the Christian era. St Tegla's Well in Clwyd and St Winifred's Well at Holywell in North Wales have already been mentioned. Owing to its geological structure, Mid-Wales boasted a selection, such as Holy Well at Pilleth, the waters of which had a reputation for the healing of diseases of the eyes. The remains of this well can still be seen in the churchyard of St Mary's Church, together with the steps that were built to make access to the well easier for pilgrims.

Some of these wells in due course developed into spas, such as Llanwrtyd Wells in Powys. This small town, which today claims to be 'ideal for exploring the wild and broken plateau of Central Wales', is built astride the river Irfon. At one time it achieved fame on account of its sulphur and chalybeate springs, the former having a higher content of sulphur than any other spa in Britain. The story of its discovery in 1732, as recorded by Francis Jones in *The Holy Wells of Wales*, has a pleasing ecclesiastical tang. 'The Rev. Theophilus Evans, who suffered from a scorbutic complaint, espied an extremely healthy-looking frog emerging from Ff. Ddrewllyd. It occurred to him that water which could produce such vitality in a frog might do similarly for a priest of the

Established Church. Where the frog had gambolled the vicar now quaffed with the results that within a few weeks he was cured.' In the same neighbourhood is Glana Wells which for a time came into the public eye, not so much for the medicinal value of its waters, but because Lady Hester Stanhope lived nearby when she retired to the Principality after the death of her favourite brother.

Trefriw ('place of healing') on the river Conway, 'this charming little Welsh health resort' as it has been described, was renowned for the high iron content of its waters, of which it was said that, 'There is probably no more valuable iron water in the British Isles.' Today they are advertised as 'so strong that you will only need to take about two tablespoonfuls per day'. Llangammarch, on the river Irfon, a tributary of the Wye, owed its reputation as a spa to the high barium chloride content (6·8 grains per gallon) of its waters, which gave them, it was claimed, a 'noteworthy and important' effect on the heart and circulation. The spring was discovered quite accidentally during the early part of the last century by a shepherd who noticed the spring issuing from the bed of the river when it was at a particularly low level.

Builth Wells, once a most fashionable spa (though its main claim to fame today is as the venue of the Royal Welsh Agricultural Show) reached the peak of its popularity in the eighteenth century, when the local gentry and 'elegant townsfolk', as they were described, could be seen parading along the promenade leading to the Park Wells on the fringe of the town. Its popularity persisted into the nineteenth century, but was gradually eclipsed by the successful exploitation of the springs at Llandrindod Wells, some 7 miles farther north.

The interest of Llandrindod Wells is that, with a history stretching back to Roman days, if not earlier, it is one of the still viable spas in the United Kingdom. It is therefore deserving of detailed consideration.

At one time known as Ffynon-llwyn y Gog (the well in the cuckoo's grove), the name of one of its springs, the town gets its present name from the old Llandrindod parish church, which dates back to the twelfth century, though it underwent considerable restoration in 1895. In passing, it is of interest that the election of the first Archbishop of Wales took place in it, and subsequent archbishops have been elected in it until quite recently when, in the words of the Curator of the Llandrindod Wells Museum, 'The Governing Body of the Church of Wales made other arrangements.'

The town as it exists today is little over a century old, but the history of the springs which were responsible for its coming into being and developing into what the Welsh Tourist Board describes as 'a great spa' (supplemented by 'the ideal touring centre of Mid-Wales') dates back into the early history of the Principality. Tradition has it that the wells are the Balnea Siluria mentioned by Pliny, and one local historian claims that, 'The old Britons, and most probably the Romans, made use of the mineral waters and used them for baths.' Certainly there are remains of a Roman fort, dating back to around A.D. 78 but, according to another, and more recent, historian: 'Although the strategic significance of the north-south trending basin of the River Ithon on the banks of which the town is built, was appreciated by both the Romans and Normans, who established an auxiliary fort and a castle at Castell Collen and Cefnyllys, respectively, neither fortification gave rise to any lasting settlement.' In more imaginative, if not romantic, strain, an 1890 guide book comments that, 'Some of the knowing ones in the present day suggest that Llandrindod and Llanwrtyd were the sites where stood Sodom and Gomorrah, which accounts for the sulphurous nature of the place.'

Be all that as it may, whatever the antiquity of the wells as a source of healing waters, and whatever the connotation of the scriptural attribution of the sulphurous spring (for which there is a possible plebeian explanation, as will be seen shortly), the 'modern' history of Llandrindod as a spa dates back to the end of the seventeenth century, when a family named Vaughan is reported as resorting to the use of the saline springs, an example followed by the other local inhabitants. In 1736, another local resident, Mrs Jenkins by name, rediscovered the saline spring of the Vaughans and at the same time discovered the sulphur spring, 'with which', it is recorded, 'she effected some important cures – a fortunate stroke which brought the place and herself into repute.'

Ten years were to elapse, however, before the efforts of the admirable Mrs Jenkins were to bear any fruit – a lag period which is scarcely surprising in view of the remoteness and inaccessibility of the spot, and the fact that at this time there was scarcely what even could be described as a village – rather less than a dozen scattered houses. In 1746, however, what must have been an enterprising Shropshire lawyer published a record entitled *A Journey to Llandrindod Wells*, plus a poem, *Parson's Tale*, based on a visit he had paid to the wells. Two years later another poem praising the waters appeared in *The Gentleman's Magazine*. This publicity caught the eye of William Grosvenor of Shrewsbury, who moved in, leased some of the existing houses, and repaired and extended them for the accommodation of visitors. In addition, he built a magnificent hotel, the Grosvenor Hotel, with accommodation for 200 visitors, complete with what has been described as 'all the amenities necessary to the fashionable society of the period': balls and assemblies, racing, and shops of all descriptions, not to mention swans in the lake overlooked by the hotel.

It flourished, achieving great popularity and attracting the gay and young. This very popularity, especially with this particular clientele, proved its undoing in the long run, and Nemesis overtook it in the form of the outbreak of hostilities with the American colonies and France, which removed many of its patrons. The reputation it achieved as a gambling haunt – and even worse – was unhelpful too. Bath might be able to get away with this sort of reputation, but not a spa in the Principality. Whether it was local criticism that prevailed, or whether the then proprietor was of a puritanical turn of mind, the hotel closed down some time after 1787 and, according to one historian, what had become 'a rendezvous chiefly for fashionable gamesters and libertines' in due course was 'razed to the ground' by its owner. Hence, possibly, an explanation of the reference to Sodom and Gomorrah already quoted.

In passing, and on a somewhat happier note, it is worthy of note that in 1805 another hotel, the Pump House Hotel, was opened on the site of the farmhouse of Mrs Jenkins, who can justly be described as the progenitor of the modern Llandrindod Wells.

Which brings us back to the spa aspect of this intriguing, if remote, Welsh centre. This had not been neglected, and it was considerably enhanced by *A Treatise on the Three Medicinal Mineral Waters at Llandrindod in Radnorshire, S. Wales*, which appeared in 1756. Written by Dr Diederick Wessel Linden, M.D., who had spent a few weeks in Llandrindod in 1754, it went into raptures about its waters, by the use of which he was 'completely restored to health'. 'Their good effects', he declaimed, 'are so conspicuous that they give place to none in Europe.' Progress, however, was slow, in spite of the fact that yet another medical man, Dr R. Williams of Aberystwyth, a pupil of Sir Astley Cooper, the famous London surgeon, wrote a pamphlet praising the springs in 1817. The main reason for this slow progress was almost certainly the seclusion and inaccessibility of the spot. As one writer has put it, 'Access for the fine establishment built by William Grosvenor of Shrewsbury left much to be desired.' So much so that, according to another account, 'All was desolation and the common a bleak inhospitable waste.'

All this, however, was to be changed by energetic intervention on the part of Sir Richard Green Price, who purchased what was known as the Rock House Estate and promoted the Central Wales Railway. In 1865, the railway station at Llandrindod was opened, and the way was all clear, after a slow start, for the development of Llandrindod as, in the words of one enthusiast, 'one of the largest – and if not largest, the best – and chief of health resorts and inland watering places in the United Kingdom,

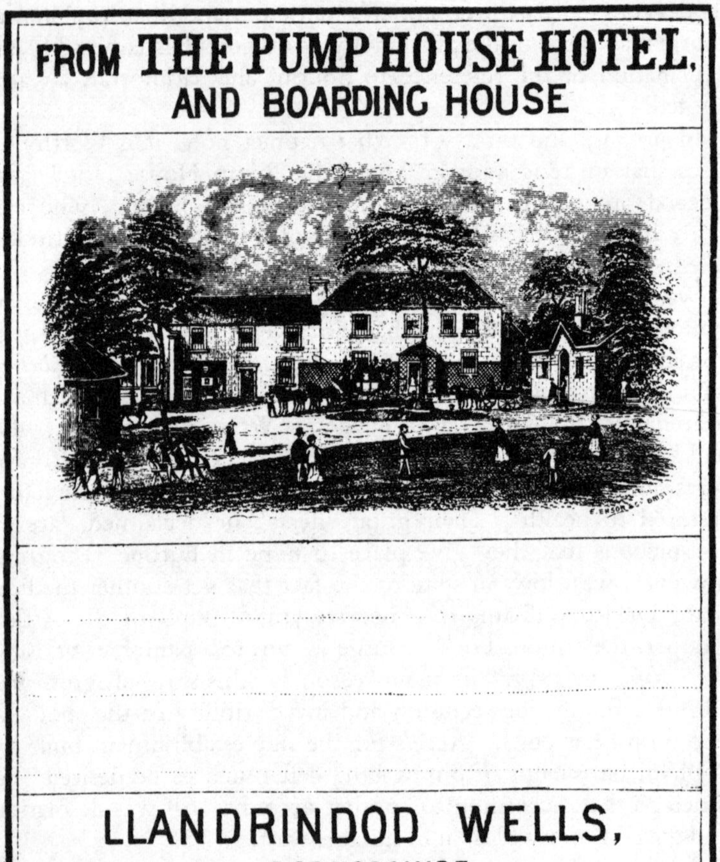

A visitor's luggage label of the mid-nineteenth century. *Llandrindod Wells Museum and the County Information Service, Powys County Council.*

yea, the "Homburg" of Great Britain.' 'Llandrindod bristled with hotels and apartments,' according to one report, 'new bath and treatment centres, a golf course, bowling and putting greens, two pavilions, one of which had accommodation for 2000, an orchestra and a 14-acre boating lake.' 'Gentility', it is noted, 'was the keynote and the Visitors' Books began to read like the pages of *Who's Who*. But the waters drew upper and middle class alike, and the Pump House Hotel, which was rebuilt in 1888, even had two tariffs to cater for first and second class visitors.' A feature of Llandrindod Wells that made it unique among spas was the visitors' prayer-meeting held every weekday morning in the Albert Hall, built in 1896 and holding some 700 people. Indeed, this was the primary purpose of the hall. That all this expansion was justified is exemplified by the fact that at its peak of popularity the spa was attracting 80,000 visitors a year.

Medically, Llandrindod, with its three types of water, chalybeate (i.e., iron containing), saline and sulphur, gushing from a multiplicity of springs, gradually developed all the appurtenances of a spa. Much of this development occurred under the watchful eye of Dr Bowen Davies, the first doctor to reside in the town, who arrived in 1872. The waters were either drunk, or used externally in baths, and in due course all the various forms of hydrotherapy and electrical treatment were installed.

For nigh on half a century after the arrival of the railway this Welsh spa maintained its popularity, attracting visitors from far and near. Many, of course, came from South Wales, which was hit so badly by the worsening economic conditions of the post-1918 era, particularly the crippling miners' strikes. This, combined with the effect of the First World War, initiated the gradual decline in its popularity, a process which was exacerbated by the Second World War. In the 1920s the Urban District Council stepped in to stop the rot, inspired primarily not by the medical value of the spa, but by its financial value as a bait for visitors to the town – then its main source of income. In a statement issued in November 1925 the Chairman of the Urban District Council,

The Pump Room at the Grand Pavilion was opened in 1912. *Llandrindod Wells Museum and the County Information Service, Powys County Council.*

after referring to the Act of Parliament authorizing the Council to provide a 'Water-drinking and Bathing Establishment', reported that the Council, 'inspired by the great success of similar Establishments carried on municipally at Bath, Harrogate, Buxton, etc.', was proposing to buy out the present private owners of the spa facilities for £26,600. This proposal, he noted, had the unanimous support of the Medical Society, the Development Association, representatives of the various principal interests in the town as well as the London Midland and Scottish Railway. His peroration is worth quoting in full: 'When the scheme of the Ministry of Health and the Friendly Societies for the treatment of insured persons at British Spas comes into operation, Llandrindod Wells will receive a full share of the patients, with consequently a regular income of thousands of pounds per annum.' The scope of these ambitions is admirably illustrated by two architect's drawings, dated 1920, of a proposed new Pump Room, to be built on a scale comparable to, if not exceeding, that of Buxton and Harrogate. As the Curator of the Llandrindod Wells Museum, in which they are housed, commented when he showed them to me, they were 'pipe dreams' of the days when the Council's hopes were running high.

The spa, however, survived, to receive another set-back from the Second World War. Ambitious plans for a new spa conceived during the war came to nought, but the coming of the National Health Service gave it a temporary boost, the arrangement being that the spa was run by the Council and paid for by the National Health Service. It had its ups and downs. In 1953, for example, it was adding 8*d.* to the rates, but in 1966, with 7,172 treatments, there was a token profit of £153. The over-all picture, however, was one of a gradual fall in the number of patients, most of whom were local inhabitants being paid for by the National Health Service, and very few private patients.

The final *coup de grâce* came in 1972, when the Right Honourable David Gibson-Watt, the Minister of State, Welsh Office, formally declared open a new physiotherapy annexe in the Llandrindod Wells Hospital. The Pump Room was leased to a private company which continued to sell the traditional spring water during the season. Few visitors come now for the sole purpose of drinking the water, but quite a few sample it as part of the holiday.

Such was the position when I visited Llandrindod Wells last autumn. It is beautifully sited 750 feet above sea level on the banks of the River Ithon, and surrounded by hills, notably Radnor Forest some 10 miles to the north-east, which afford protection from most of the prevailing winds. The first impression is one of *déja vu*, a somewhat disturbing experience until one suddenly realizes that the spacious houses, so unexpected in a relatively small township at the back of beyond, are reminiscent of other well-known spas such as Bath and Buxton. Not that it has a fraction of the aesthetic architectural attraction of the former, but it follows the same principle: crescents of imposing houses which were filled with visitors during the season when the town was a 'great spa'.

Rock Park, in which is the Pump Room, is pleasantly laid out in a natural manner, being mainly woodland with many walks, some of which lead down to the Ithon. The Pump Room, which was closed when I was there as the season was over, was not as neat and tidy as it might have been, but far from neglected. Nearby is the chalybeate spring, known as the Rock Sprout, above which is a granite stone bearing the following superscription:

THIS FOUNTAIN AND THE FREE CHALYBEATE SPRING WERE GIVEN FOR THE USE OF THE PUBLIC BY THE LORD OF THE MANOR, J. W. GIBSON, ESQ., 1879

It is of more than passing interest that the donor was a great-grandson of James Watt, the engineer of steam-engine fame, and that *his* grandson should have formally opened the hospital annexe that replaced the spa in 1972.

As I approached the spring I found its water being sampled by a middle-aged man, obviously a victim of Parkinsonism. When I got into conversation with him, he told me that he 'lived down the line', and whenever he could he came to Llandrindod Wells to drink the water from this spring. When I asked him whether it did him any good, his reply was that he always felt better after drinking it. Which struck me as fair comment. After all if the patient feels better, who is to argue with him? Further, this particular 'medicine' cost him nothing (a fact to which he drew my attention), and was much safer and freer from side-effects than many of the potent remedies used today for the relief of this distressing condition. The effect of the chalybeate spring of Llandrindod Wells may only have been psychological but, if it brought at least a degree of comfort, that was always something.

He insisted on my sampling the water, presenting me with one of the several plastic cups he had, to do so. The water, described by an 1896 commentator as 'a most useful tonic without any astringent properties' to be taken in a dosage of 2 to 10 fluid ounces three times a day after meals, came out clear and had rather a salty, not unpleasant, taste.

My over-all impression was that Llandrindod Wells is still a viable spa if only someone with initiative would come along and develop it. The Pump Room is still in existence and, although the company to which it was leased has gone bankrupt, another company, I was told, had taken it over and was proposing to develop it as a sports centre.

The town itself is far from decadent and bemoaning its past. It has been selected as one of six 'growth towns' of Mid-Wales, and is the administrative centre of the new county of Powys, which came into being under the 1974 local authority reorganization by the merger of Montgomeryshire, Radnorshire and most of Breconshire. With that appropriate sense of historical continuity so typical of the Welsh, the offices of the new county authority are housed in the former Pump Room Hotel, once the centre of social life and built on the site of the farmhouse of Mrs Jenkins, the founding mother of the spa.

The town, with a population of around 3500, is still a popular holiday resort and had over 35,000 visitors in 1975. It has an annual Drama Festival, which has been described as 'the most notable annual event of the kind in Wales', and it houses the annual Welsh Semi-National Eisteddfod. It is developing as a conference centre, as I learned from personal experience when on my last night my hotel was packed out with salesmen attending a conference over the weekend. There is a conference hall which can seat 600 delegates, as well as 500 seats in the aforementioned Albert Hall. There may not be as many hotels as at one time, but one at least has 140 rooms. A further point to be borne in mind is that, in spite of many threats, the railway is still functioning – on the Western Region line from Llanelli to Shrewsbury.

In other words, Llandrindod Wells has all the holiday attractions, and the ease of access, which form such an integral part of a successful spa. With these superadded to the existing spa facilities, which are fully capable of development, there is no reason why it should not regain its old glory and provide a first-class spa for the inhabitants of the Principality so far as the National Health Service is concerned, and for many from farther afield as private patients, seeking relief from their rheumatic aches and pains.

Advertisement of 1881

13

Scottish spas

'Scottish spas' seems almost a contradiction in terms. Caledonia, stern and wild, scarcely lends itself as a congenial background to the amenities and comforts of a spa. With one notable exception, spas are not part of the national heritage north of the Tweed, but Scotland did cash in on the concept last century by developing a string of hydropathics, as they were known, some of which still exist, though little more than hotels today. These are dealt with in the chapter on hydrotherapy. The one exception is Strathpeffer, which is of interest, not only for historical reasons, but also because there is no good reason why it could not be revived as a useful and viable spa.

'Set like a Jewel 'mid the splendours of the North', Strathpeffer (valley of the radiant river), situated 24 miles north-west of Inverness, has been variously described as the 'focal point of tourist Scotland', 'the Harrogate of Scotland' and 'the Harrogate of the Highlands'. Amongst its main attributes is that of possessing an 'uncommonly mild and sunny winter climate'. Beautifully sited in a strath, or valley, and protected from the prevailing west winds by the 3500-foot Ben Wyvis, it is certainly one of the most attractive of Highland villages. Indeed, there is much justification for the comment that, 'It has more the appearance of a Swiss village.' 'Set like a Jewel 'mid the splendours of the North' is no figment of the poetic imagination, as I learned when I visited it in November. Even the weather lined up with the claim made for it, being mild and sunny, with a softness one associates more with the clime of southern England.

Its history is as tempestuous and bloodthirsty as that of any part of Scotland, particularly north of the Forth and Clyde. 'From earliest times', as has been noted, 'the district around Strathpeffer has been a natural settlement. Lake dwellers, pre-Christian religious sects, sun-worshippers, all have left their records in the form of rock carvings, stone circles, burial mounds, standing stones and crannogs.' Almost inevitably it has its holy well. Originally known as the Saint's Well, it is now referred to more prosaically as the Iron Well, presumably because its waters arise from one of the chalybeate springs. It is said to have been esteemed by a holy man who had his cell nearby. Whether or not it has any association with St Duthus, the patron saint of Ross-shire, is not known.

How far back in history these wells were used for their healing virtues is also unknown, but certainly for many centuries the locals used them for the rheumatics. The modern history of Strathpeffer as a spa dates from 1772 when Dr Donald Monro, F.R.S., physician to St George's Hospital, London, read a communication to the Royal Society, on what he referred to as the 'Castle Leod Water' – so called after the one-time residence of the Earls of Cromartie, which is near the spa. In this he quotes a Dr Alexander Mackenzie of Tarbet as saying: 'Every person in the country prescribes the water for themselves and runs to the well or sends for the water for every complaint, acute and chronic.' Others had informed him that the waters 'had been used with success in curing the itch', and his general conclusion was: 'It appears that this is one of the strongest sulphureous waters hitherto found in Britain . . . Equal parts of the Castle Leod and sea water mixed together makes a water in most respect similar to the Harrogate: and probably will be found to answer in most cases where the Harrogate water has been found useful.'

Five years later, in view of the increasing number of visitors induced by this publicity, Mr Colin Mackenzie, the local factor, petitioned the Commissioners of Forfeited Estates (the Estate of Cromartie, which included Strathpeffer, had been one of the many forfeited following the 1745 rebellion) for permission to build near the 'fine Mineral Well', as he described it, 'a good House, Kitchen and Stable' which would be 'a great accommodation to those frequenting the Well', adding prophetically: 'Nor is it improbable that in time this place might become a thriving village.' In the course of his petition he reported that the parish minister had 'caused to be erected a kind of building about this Well to preserve it from being abused by cattle, etc., which by no means answers the end proposed'. This still further publicized the well and the additional investigation which it induced revealed that there were several springs of both chalybeate and sulphur water.

Progress, however, was still slow. In his delightfully quaint book, *Strathpeffer Spa. Its Climate and Waters* published in 1889, Dr Fortescue Fox, one of the leading spa specialists of the time and the founder-father of Strathpeffer Spa in its Victorian and Edwardian days, attributes this to the difficulty of access, recording that, 'Old men still alive remember the month's journey from London with the Laird's coach.' Things began to pick up again as a result of the efforts of Dr Morrison of Dunsaig, in Aberdeenshire, who came to Strathpeffer for treatment for his crippling rheumatoid arthritis which had resisted all other forms of treatment. Having obtained a 'complete cure' from the use of the sulphur water, he settled in the village with a view to 'putting Strathpeffer on a par with Harrogate and Bath among the spas of Britain', and was instrumental in having a small Pump Room built over what was known as the 'Strong Well' in 1819. It was not really, however, until the railway reached Strathpeffer in 1885 that it attained its full status as a spa.

From then until 1914 Strathpeffer was a popular and fashionable spa, to which people came from all over Britain. Its sulphur waters, with their high content of 19 cubic inches of sulphuretted hydrogen per gallon (compared with 10 in the Harrogate waters), was used both internally (for dyspepsia, 'tropical' liver, and kidney disease) and externally in the form of baths for gout, all forms of rheumatism and some chronic forms of skin disease such as eczema and psoriasis. The chalybeate waters were used internally for anaemia and as a tonic. The interesting thing is that this late-Victorian list of indications for the use of the water is very comparable with the uses of both a century earlier and those in a list published after the First World War.

A noteworthy feature of Strathpeffer is that it was the first British spa to use peat baths. The disintegrated peat, of which there are enormous deposits on the shoulders of Ben Wyvis, was used either as a plain peat bath or in combination with the sulphur water for 'its effect as a thermal agency on obstinate skin affections, and more especially for its effect in promoting the absorption of exudations in affections of the joints'. Pine baths were also given. The scope of the spa in those halcyon days is vividly exemplified in the advertisement from a Victorian guide book.

Although the spa never regained its pre-1914 popularity, it was still in active existence in 1919, as shown by the following extracts from a book on British spas published that year. 'The town itself is a small one [population of 3000 in the season], practically wholly given up to the interests of the spa . . . There is a pump room, with a fairly well-equipped bath installation . . . The waters from four different springs are employed . . . The course is from three to five weeks.'

Today, alas, 'every prospect pleases', as I found out on a recent visit, except the spa. According to a letter I have had from one of the directors of the company owning the two major hotels, 'Unfortunately, some years ago the main pump-room was, for reasons unknown to me, demolished and in this building were the sulphur baths. Sulphur or peat baths are no longer available and in the season the small pump-room is open for the waters and only available for drinking. The iron content waters are not readily

THE

HIGHLAND SULPHUR SPA,

STRATHPEFFER, ROSS-SHIRE.

These Waters are among the strongest in Europe, and are unrivalled in Great Britain in the treatment of

CHRONIC RHEUMATISM

DISEASES OF THE SKIN,

AND

AFFECTIONS OF THE LIVER AND KIDNEYS.

Superior Effervescing Chalybeate Spring,

UNIQUE IN THIS COUNTRY.

SULPHUR BATHS AND DOUCHES HEATED ON THE MOST APPROVED SYSTEM.

EXTENSIVE IMPROVEMENTS AND ALTERATIONS EFFECTED SINCE LAST SEASON.

SPLENDID PAVILION FOR BALLS, CONCERTS, ETC.

Resident Physician—Dr. FORTESCUE FOX, from London Hospital.

See Late Dr. MANSON'S Book, 5th Edition.

IMPROVED DRAINAGE AND WATER SUPPLY.

STRATHPEFFER.

BEN WYVIS HOTEL,

Two Minutes walk from Railway Station and

MINERAL WELLS AND BATHS,

CONTAINS SPLENDID NEW DRAWING AND DINING ROOMS,

PUBLIC AND PRIVATE APARTMENTS

(*En Suite*),

BILLIARD AND RECREATION ROOMS,

BOWLING AND TENNIS GREENS,

Amidst Scenery Unsurpassed in Scotland.

NEAR POST AND TELEGRAPH OFFICES.

POSTING. **APPLY THE MANAGER.**

A late-nineteenth century advertisement for Strathpeffer. *Where Shall We Go?* (London).

available due to the pipes corroding over the years.' The village, however, is still very much alive and as attractive as ever, with a relatively high proportion of hotels. 'It is delightfully picturesque' (here I quote from the 1919 publication previously alluded to), 'Scotch firs, spruce, and larch abound, along with many flowers... The rainfall is but 30 inches, much lower than in places to the west of the spa. There is quite a remarkable amount of sunshine for so northerly a district.'

There is a small local hospital and there is no reason why this should not become the centre of a modern Pump Room complex, which is all that is required to convert it into a modern spa. Its virtually unique waters are simply flowing to waste at the moment, and there is no reason why it should not become the Highland Spa under the aegis of the Highland Health Board. Not only is there the small local Nicolson Mackenzie Hospital in Strathpeffer itself, but also a 40-bedded hospital in Dingwall, which is only 6 miles away, and two excellent hospitals in Inverness, 24 miles away, which could provide expert rheumatological opinions. In addition, a modern efficient spa would be an irresistible attraction for private patients from all over the United Kingdom, fully justifying part of the lavish grants for development of the Highlands being devoted to the resurrection of this admirable spa that healed – and would continue to do so if only it were given the chance. As Cuthbert Graham points out in his recently published *Portrait of the Moray Firth*, 'if the population increases envisaged for the Cromarty Firth industrial area materialize, there will certainly be a future for the old spa'.

Scotland's only other spa in the strict sense of the term, was at Moffat, in Dumfries-shire in the upper part of the Vale of Annan, some 60 miles south of Edinburgh and 2 miles from Beattock Junction, so well known to railway travellers in the old days of the Caledonian Railway. Its name is said to be derived from the Gaelic *Oua-vat*, a long deep mountain hollow, characteristically translated by a twentieth century writer as a coal-scoop. The town has one of the broadest High Streets in Scotland.

The Pump Room, Strathpeffer. *Fodderty W.R.I.*

Moffat Well, as it is known, which is a mile and a half out of the town, was discovered in 1633 by Rachel Whiteford, daughter of the Bishop of Brechin, the owner of considerable estates in and around the parish of Moffat. It had the curious experience of being introduced, in 1659, to the public in Latin, in a work entitled *Fons Moffetensis: seu Descriptio Topographico-Spagyrica Fontium Mineralium Moffetensium, in Annandia Scotia* – as pretty an example of dog Latin as ever came out of a Scottish pedant's head. In spite of, or because of, this effort the Well was not long in attracting attention. Thus, in 1660, it is recorded, the 12-year-old Countess of Buccleuch was recommended to take the Waters for an illness of 'heterogeneous nature', including a running sore. Unfortunately neither this nor the Royal Touch from Charles II had any effect and she died of measles the following year.

As a spa it really began to come to life following a series of reports by medical men, including Professor Andrew Plummer, Professor of Medicine in the University of Edinburgh in the latter part of the eighteenth century, and an analysis of the waters, showing their high sulphur content, by Professor Thomas Thomson, Professor of Chemistry in the University of Glasgow in 1828.

By the latter half of the eighteenth century it had become quite a well-known watering resort, attracting, amongst others, a coterie of literary men, including David Hume, the historian, Joseph Black, the chemist, and James Boswell. Robert Burns was also a regular visitor. Of Boswell one of his biographers records that he 'was sent for a cure to the watering-place of Moffat, then a small village with none of the amenities of the famous English watering-places, but popular for its sulphur springs . . . The countryside, the springs (he both drank and bathed in the water) and the company seem to have combined to restore his health.'

According to the 17th edition of *Black's Picturesque Tourist of Scotland*, published in 1865, Moffat was then 'noted for its mineral waters and as a healthy summer residence. The mineral spring called Moffat Well is situated on the side of a beautiful linn a mile and a half from the village. The water is sulphureous, and when taken from the spring has a strong disagreeable smell and slightly saline taste.' A decade later the Ex-Empress Eugénie of France was a frequent visitor, and it is to this period also (1879) that dates the foundation by the father of Air Chief Marshal Lord Dowding of the well-known preparatory school, St Ninian's, where his famous son was born.

A 1902 account indicates that there was still considerable activity, recording that during the season the road to the Well 'usually presents a very lively appearance with omnibuses, private carriages, pedestrians and cyclists on their way to or returning from the spring'. Of this it is said that, 'A small stone building covers the well.' In parenthesis it is noted that 'Two very apt quotations from Horace were inscribed on two of the stones of the building originally erected over the well, but they have now disappeared. The first was:

Aeque pauperibus prodest, locupletibus aeque. 1 Epist. i. 25
(It does good alike to the poor and the rich.)

The other:

Infirmo capiti fluit utilis, utilis alvo. 1 Epist. xvi. 14
(It flows beneficial to the infirm head, beneficial to the bowels.)'

Beside this building the description continues, 'stands a neat wooden shed or "verandah" for the accommodation of visitors . . . On the green adjoining the well stands an old building called "The Ball-room", from the use for which it was formerly employed.'

By 1919 it was obviously much in decline, a report in that year stating that 'Moffat makes some claim to be a spa, as there is the famous well about a mile and a half out of the town. The spring is sulphurous and muriated, but with low mineralization . . . The sulphur water is markedly diuretic in effect and is of service in gout and rheumatism etc. Some skin conditions seem to benefit from the outward application.' The decline was speeded up in 1921, when the large Hydropathic Hotel, built at the end of the nineteenth century, followed the current example of so many Scottish hotels and went up in flames.

Today it is merely a small unpretentious country town, attractive as a convenient centre for touring the southern uplands of Scotland, than which there is no fairer land in the British Isles.

Two other 'spas' are worthy of note, not for their medical interest, but for their literary associations. One is Brow Well situated on the edge of the Solway Firth a mile and a half southwest of the village of Clarencefield on the Dumfries to Annan road. Its only claim to fame is that Robert Burns was sent to it on 3 July 1796, in his terminal illness, by his medical adviser, Dr Maxwell, 'to indulge', in the words of Catherine Carswell in her *Life of Robert Burns*, 'in sea-bathing, horse exercise, glasses of port wine and iron water', not to mention mercury and laudanum, as Mr J. A. C. McFadden, the secretary of the Dumfries Burns Club reminded me. This pathetic terminal episode in Burns' life is best told in Mrs Carswell's words.

> 'Because it had a spring of mild chalybeate water, which was contained in a red stone tank the size of a kitchen table, the place was dignified by the name of a spa . . . But provision for a sick man there was none. It was a mean, dilapidated, dismal little clachan, consisting of a dozen cottages and an inn that was no more than a cottage. For the spa some rickety benches in a broken shed did duty, and a 20-yard "esplanade" of tufted sea-grass. Throughout the cold grey July it was unutterably cheerless . . . Each day he waded shakily – he had to wade a long way to get the required depth – into the chill Atlantic water that he might stand obediently up to his armpits till it was time to drag his aching joints out again and slowly dry himself and sip his allowance of port.'

He stuck it out until 18 July and then, with the homing instinct of a dying animal, made for Dumfries, where he died on 21 July.

Not inappropriately, before he died he was able to write his last song, '"Oh" Wert Thou in the Cauld Blast'.

Brow Well was never a spa in the precise term of the word: i.e., that it had commercial springs and accommodation for visitors. Mr Desmond Donaldson, Regional Librarian of the Dumfries and Galloway Regional Council, writing in response to my seeking his advice on the matter, tells me that so far as he can make out, 'It was just a little natural well with a reputation locally. One of the tiny nearby houses may have been classified as an "inn". Because of the connexion with Burns a little brick wall has been built around the well of water, but it is an extremely miserable and deserted-looking spot today.'

The other Scottish spa with literary associations is St Ronan's Well at Innerleithen, which owes its popularity to Sir Walter Scott. This association, though somewhat far fetched and entirely fortuitous, provides a happier story than the one just retailed. It begins paradoxically in England at a place in Cumbria called Gilsland, which lies on the banks of the river Irthing where it separates the one-time counties of Northumberland and Cumberland. Here are sulphur springs that were patronized by the Romans and in due course received the blessing of the Christian Church and given the name of Holy Well. Time passed and the Holy Well developed into a spa which would never have achieved more than local patronage if Sir Walter Scott had not stayed at the thatched Schaws Hotel, which was built in 1700. Here he met Charlotte Carpenter, his future wife. As was inevitable, Gilsland was to crop up in his novels: *Guy Mannering* and *St Ronan's Well*, and it was the latter that brought fame to Innerleithen.

Before reverting to Innerleithen, however, the Gilsland Spa story may be completed. According to the *Directory of Cumberland and Westmorland*, 1829, for a reference to which I am grateful to Mrs Mary Allison of the Brampton Tourist Information Centre, 'Few watering-places are so bountifully gifted by nature as this.' It noted that there were four springs – one, the original one, sulphurous; the other three, discovered in 1812, chalybeate in nature – 'All of which may be employed, either externally or internally, in a diversity of disease, with great success.' The coming of the railway in 1838 was a godsend and by the middle of the century the Spa was at the height of its fame. The original hotel was burned down in 1859, to be replaced by a larger one, built in 1865, which Sir Nikolaus Pevsner describes as 'an ambitious spa Hotel'. Today the hotel is a convalescent home, but Mrs Allison tells me that, 'Spa water is still available from the well in the very pleasant woodland adjoining the Gilsland Spa Hotel.'

In his introduction to *St Ronan's Well*, the author states: 'The scene chosen for the author's little drama of modern life was a mineral spring such as are to be found in both divisions of Britain.' In the Author's Notes the following appears: 'St Ronan's, since this veracious history was given to the public, has revived as a sort of *alias*, or second title, to the very pleasant village of Innerleithen upon Tweed, where there is a medicinal spring much frequented by visitors.' This last comment is amplified by Lockhart in his life of his father-in-law:

> 'It [*St Ronan's Well*] was rapturously hailed by the inhabitants of Innerleithen who immediately identified the most striking of its localities with those of their own pretty village and picturesque neighbourhood and foresaw in this celebration a chance of restoring the popularity of their long neglected *Well*: – the same to which Sir Walter Scott had occasionally escorted his mother and sister in the days of boyhood. The notabilities of the little town voted by acclamation that the old name of Innerleithen should be, as far as possible, dropped thenceforth, and that of St Ronan's adopted. Nor were they mistaken in their auguries. An unheard-of influx of water-imbibers forthwith crowned their hopes.'

According to Hesketh Pearson in his biography of Scott, *Walter Scott. His Life and Personality*, 'Within a year or two it was wealthy, famous, vigorous and revolting.' Within three years of the publication of the novel, Lord Traquair, the local laird, had provided a pump-house, complete with reading-room.

What I have not been able to discover is why the scene of Scott's novel came to be associated with Innerleithen. It is fairly clear that the scene depicted is that of Gilsland, which is nothing remotely resembling Innerleithen. One possibility is Scott's love of the Scottish border country. He may well have quietly thrown out the association of ideas and, when it was enthusiastically taken up by the commercially-minded inhabitants of Innerleithen, agreed by silence, never actually saying that there was any association but allowing silence to imply agreement. Another factor may have been the well-known fact that Scott based many of the people and places in his novels on actual places and people. One result of this was that there soon developed what can only be described as a craze, among knowledgeable critics and ignoramuses alike, to go through his novels with a fine toothcomb to detect such links between fiction and actuality.

Today, Innerleithen is neither 'revolting', nor 'very pleasant' as Scott described it. It is a plain little township dominated in every sense by its hosiery and three spinning mills, in picturesque surroundings on the bank of the Tweed where it is joined by the Leithen. The Dow Well, as it was originally known, Mr P. Taylor, the Peebles Area Librarian tells me, 'from the circumstance that before its medical qualities were discovered, the perspicacious pigeons of the locale use it as place of resort', ('dow' being a Scottish term for dove or pigeon) is sited on the slope of the hill called Lee Penn overlooking the township, and today little is done to publicize it. Indeed, I had considerable difficulty in finding it when I visited Innerleithen. The water, which contains 'carbonate of magnesia, muriate of lime and muriate of soda', is led to a somewhat ornate house where it can be drunk from a tap. The spring is in the garden at the back of the house. I passed the house on the first occasion as it was so distinctively ornate, suggesting to me that it might be the residence of the provost (always assuming that there was one), and there was no indication what it was. When I finally discovered it, I was kindly received by the keeper's wife, sampled the not unpleasant-tasting water and paid my respects to the garden spring. I was told that there is still a steady stream of visitors during the season, which was evident from the visitors' book which I was asked to sign. I was also told that some of the trees around the house had been planted by Sir Walter Scott. This I have been unable to confirm, even though it is quite possible as Scott was a regular visitor to the St Ronan's Games which were instituted as a publicity gimmick to maintain the popularity of the township. In addition, as Hesketh Pearson has put it, 'The planting of trees became a mania with him,' and, while this 'mania' was concentrated on Abbotsford, where he planted five hundred acres with trees, it is not in the least unlikely that he might have planted some around the Well to which he had brought such fame.

An interesting association between the Well and the Games of St Ronan developed in the form of a regular ritual, for the following description of which I am indebted to Mr Taylor: 'The final part of the ritual takes place on the last day of the Games, a Saturday, when a torchlight procession carries an effigy of the Devil to the top of Caerless, by the Well, and consigns him to a great bonfire. This commemorates St Ronan, a seventh-century monk, whose vigorous way with the superstitious of his time was symbolically displayed by showing the monk with his crozier "cleiking the deil" by the hind leg.' An interesting phenomenon in the home of Presbyterianism and the land of John Knox.

Thus ends this strange eventful historical mystery – a tribute to the popularity and influence of the wizard of Abbotsford and the financial perspicacity of the citizens of Innerleithen.

14

Hydrotherapy & hydropathics

Hydrotherapy has been defined as 'the external application of water for therapeutic purposes'. It is one of the oldest forms of therapy, having been practised all down the ages, as described in chapter 1. Indeed, as has been noted, 'There are few therapeutic agents that have been used continuously for thousands of years in virtually the same form and whose popularity has increased. Water is one of these agents.' Whilst hydrotherapy is an integral part of spa therapy, it has also been, and is, practised on its own, and it is this aspect that will be discussed in this chapter.

The father of modern British hydrotherapy was Sir John Floyer, the Lichfield physician who, in 1647, published a work entitled *An Inquiry into the Right Use of the Hot, Cold and Temperate Baths in England*, followed by *History of Cold Baths* in 1715, both of which have been described as 'classics in the history of hydrotherapy'. He was by no means a 'voice crying in the wilderness', for a senior contemporary, John Locke, the physician and philosopher, was a strong advocate of the strengthening property of cold water.

It was in Germany and the Austro-Hungarian Empire, however, that hydrotherapy was to develop into a craze that swept over the greater part of Northern and Central Europe and ultimately spread to North America. Its principal popularizer was

Vincent Priessnitz (1799–1851) who has been described as 'a simple Silesian peasant'. He may have been simple from the academic point of view, but he had all the traditional shrewdness of the peasant. As a young man he was run over by a wagon and so severely injured that he was told by his surgeon that he would be an invalid for life. This gloomy prognosis he refused to accept, and, it is recorded by Professor Ralph Major the eminent American medical historian, 'by keeping wet compresses on his chest for a year and drinking large quantities of water, recovered completely'. What could cure him, he then argued, could obviously cure others and, in the words of Professor Major, 'At the age of 18 he instituted his water cure for disease, a treatment which soon found many adherents among the high and the low, the rich and the poor.'

Thousands flocked to him at Grafenberg, in Silesia, to undergo what his critics described as his 'crude' and 'fanatical' method of hydrotherapy. 'Crude', or 'fanatical' it may have been – cold baths lasting for hours, the drinking of vast quantities of water, and various forms of exercise, including the sawing of logs for heating the premises – but it worked. In a way he was fortunate in his timing. The ever-emotional and impressionable German was in one of his moods of emotional elation and indulging in a new craze, or orgy, known as *Naturarzt*, or natural medicine: one of the many back-to-Nature campaigns that infiltrate Teutonic civilization periodically. This particular outbreak was characterized, as it has been put, by 'mystical tendencies, homoeopathy and teaching of the futility of drugs'. Among those who visited him, sampled his treatment, and were converted to it, were two British citizens who were to be responsible for introducing his technique to England: Dr James Wilson and Hamer Stansfield. But before moving back to our 'ain' country, passing reference must be made to Pastor Sebastian Kneipp (1821–1897), the Bavarian whose 'cure' was still practised in 1959 in West Germany, where there were 27 Kneipp health resorts and 900 doctors who had taken training in the method. This consists basically of alternating cold and warm applications of water in various forms, combined with a largely vegetarian diet and regular exercise including 'early mornings treading barefoot in the dewy grass for one to five minutes or barefoot treading in the snow for a half to one minute'.

So successful was this 'natural medicine' movement that it began to affect the pockets of orthodox German doctors and, as successive British Ministers of Health have found to their cost in recent years, there is no more effective method of stirring up medical opposition than in this way. So upset were the German doctors that a commission was set up, under Professor Adolf Kussmaul (1822–1902), one of the most distinguished German physicians of his day, to investigate to what extent the medical curriculum should be modified to overcome this unorthodox trespassing, by peasant and priest, on the territory of orthodox medicine. The following excerpt from the commission's report, with its topical ring, is of more than passing interest.

> 'There is no doubt that trust in the prescription is waning among educated people and that the confidence in dietetic remedies and in the remedial value of water is in the ascendant. Water has especially won for itself steadily growing confidence as a remedy. Hydrotherapy combined with diet may, undoubtedly, bring about or aid in the cure of numberless acute and chronic diseases. Of hydrotherapy the young physician knows nothing when he leaves the university. Unhappily, he sooner or later may encounter discomfiture when an uneducated water-doctor steps in and cures the patient after he has failed. Herein lies a great gap in the education of our physicians.'

It was one of these 'water-doctors', though neither uneducated nor German, who was to put hydrotherapy on the English therapeutic map. This was Dr James Wilson who, with Dr James Manby Gully, settled in Malvern in 1842 and earned for it the title of the 'metropolis of the water cure'. Malvern, or rather the Malverns, for they are a group of villages or towns, lies on the slopes of the Malvern Hills, said to be the oldest land in England, if not the oldest mountain range in Europe. The highest point of the 9-mile long range of hills is the Worcestershire Beacon, and, as has been said, 'From its height of 1400 feet there is to be obtained not only one of the most extensive views in Great Britain, but also one of the most picturesque and varied.'

Its water is said to be the purest in Britain, though this claim has recently been challenged by Loch Katrine which is reputed by some experts to have the purest water in Europe. Be that as it may, the reputation of Malvern water has been commercialized for over three centuries. According to a piece of doggerel attributed to the vicar of Malvern in the reign of James I:

> Some of them into Kent,
> Some are to London sent,
> Others to Berwick went,
> Oh, praise the Lord!

In 1780 it was being sold in the streets of London for one shilling a bottle, and today around a million bottles are sold annually throughout the world. One of its regular patrons is the Queen who, it is said, goes nowhere without her Malvern Water, familiar to so many of her subjects, at home and overseas, in its red-capped bottles.

Medicinally its very purity is against it though, according to the *Breviary of The Eyes*, published in 1622, the water of the Eye Well (now silted up) had a reputation as an eye cure; hence its name. The Holy Well at Malvern Wells was visited by Evelyn, the diarist, in 1654, who reported that it 'was said to heal many infirmities, as King's evil, leprosy, sore eyes, etc.', while a decade later the first volume of the *Transactions of the Royal Society* referred to 'a long and old fame for healing of eyes'. St Anne's Well, which had a similar reputation, and was referred to by the Bishop of Worcester in 1282, is said to be the first habitation and hermitage in Great Malvern. It lies on the eastern slopes of the Hills and is reached from Great Malvern by a flight of 95 steps.

In 1815, a cottage was built over the well to provide shelter, glasses to drink the water and room 'to put the affected part under the spout', according to the current guide book. The original cottage can still be seen today. Over the 'spout' is a marble tablet presented by Lady Emily Foley in October 1892, bearing the following superscription by Rev. W. Blake:

> Drink of this crystal fountain
> And praise the loving Lord
> Who from the rocky mountain
> This living stream out-poured
> For emblem of the holy fount
> That flows from God's eternal mount.

Doggerel seems to have been a speciality of the local clergy.

The founder of Malvern as a 'spa' was Dr John Wall (1708–1776), a Worcester physician who was a co-founder of the Worcester Royal Infirmary and of the world-famous Worcester Porcelain Company. How his interest came to be aroused in Malvern as a potential spa is not clear. Some suggest that it was to allow its waters to be available for his infirmary patients. Others consider that as a loyal son of his county in the hey-day of spas he felt that Worcestershire should have one of its own. Whatever the reason, he had the water analysed. This revealed its purity for the first time, thereby being responsible for yet another of the doggerels with which Malvern seems to be beset.

> The Malvern water, says Dr Wall
> Is famed for containing just nothing at all.

This, however, did not put him off and with the aid of a committee of Worcestershire 'gentry' he had new accommodation built, starting off with a bath house by the Holy Well at Malvern Wells in 1757, and walks along the slopes of the Hills.

After Dr Wall's death, Malvern continued as what has been described as a 'minor spa', with a reputation high enough, however, to bring the Duchess of Kent, with her 12-year-old daughter, Victoria, in 1831 for a stay of several months. (A visit which Malvern commemorated at the Jubilee in 1895 by building the toposcope on the top of Worcestershire Beacon.)

Eleven years later Malvern was to undergo a metamorphosis which placed it well to the fore as *the* centre for hydrotherapy in the United Kingdom. This was the result of the coming together of two ambitious young doctors: James Manly Gully (the father of a future Speaker of the House of Commons) and James Wilson. When they first met in 1837 the latter had just returned from a visit to Grafenberg where he had studied under Vincent Priessnitz, and become an enthusiast for hydrotherapy. He infected Gully with his enthusiasm and they ultimately chose Malvern as a suitable place in which to turn their notions into profits. Wilson arrived first and at a cost of £18,000 built a prestigious hydropathic establishment, appropriately named Priessnitz House. When Gully arrived his seat of activity was two neighbouring buildings, one for men and one for women, connected by what came to be known as 'The Bridge of Sighs', as only Dr Gully could pass from the male to the female establishment.

They were an almost immediate success, rigorous though their regime was. 'Cold packs of damp sheets and blankets, sitz baths, douches, abdominal compresses and such like', according to one commentator, 'were accompanied by a spartan diet relieved only by draughts of the local waters. Alcohol, tea and coffee were taboo.' Patients were wrapped in wet sheets at 6 am and then sent up the hills, complete with alpenstock, before breakfast at St Anne's Well. (This wet-sheeting – a basic feature of the Priessnitz regime – it is interesting to note, is said to have been practised in the Middle Ages by the monks of Malvern Priory.) Among the clientele at Malvern were Carlyle, Dickens, Charles Darwin, Florence Nightingale and Bishop Wilberforce. To what extent Carlyle's views epitomized those of his fellow-visitors may be an open question but, as expressed in a letter to Emerson in 1851, from Great Malvern, they are of more than passing interest.

Dr James Manly Gully. *National Portrait Gallery, London.*

> 'It is above three weeks since my wife and I left London . . . and came hither with the purpose of a month of what is called "water cure"; for which this place, otherwise extremely pleasant and wholesome, has become celebrated of late years. Dr Gully, the pontiff of the business in our Island, warmly encouraged my purpose as soon as he heard of it; nay, urgently offered at once that both of us should become his own guests till the experiment were tried; and here accordingly we are; I water-curing, assiduously walking in the sunny mountains, drinking of the clear wells, not to speak of wet wrappings, solitary *steepages*, and other singular procedures . . . It is a strange quasi-monastic – godless yet *devotional* – way of life which human creatures have here, and is useful to them beyond doubt. I foresee this "water cure" under better forms, will become a Ramadham of the overworked underbelieving English in time to come, an institution they were dreadfully in want for, this long while.'

Darwin, who arrived, complete with wife, children and servants, after studying Gully's *The Water Cure in Chronic Disease*, published in 1846 (it ran to nine editions), was somewhat more sceptical. 'It is a sad flaw I cannot but think in my beloved Dr Gully that he believes in everything;' but his faith in the water cure was sufficient to continue with the wet-sheeting procedure, his butler acting as bathman, on his return to his home at Down.

Needless to say, this success aroused considerable opposition from the orthodox medical profession, a leading critic being Sir Charles Hastings, the founder of the British Medical Association. Financially they probably had 'good' reason for envy, for at the height of his career Gully alone was netting around £10,000 a year. As all too often happens in medical partnerships, the two incompatible doctors fell out, but there were plenty to carry on the good work. Notable among these was Dr Edward Johnson, one of whose claims to fame is that he used seventy-four different techniques of bathing and friction treatment, thus epitomizing *in excelsis* the variety in treatment gradually introduced by Gully's and Wilson's successors. Another outstanding figure was Dr R. B. Grindford, who combined his treatment with temperance on the strictest lines, thereby appealing to the temperance and nonconformist section of the population. So well did he come to be known both as an apostle of water drinking and as a water physician, that the Archbishop of Canterbury conferred on him the honorary degree of M.D. Dr Andrew Henderson is also worthy of mention. He started life as a bathman under Dr Joseph Weiss, a German associate of Priessnitz, in due course settling in England under Dr Gully. He subsequently qualified at St George's Hospital and returned to practise in Malvern where, it is recorded, 'He took more and more to the use of brandy and salt in conjunction with water and was successful with elderly people when other practitioners had failed,' thus exemplifying the Cleopatrian 'infinite variety' of hydrotherapy as practised amid the beauties of Malvern.

An outbreak of typhoid fever in 1905 cast a temporary cloud over the pure water of Malvern, but it recovered, though tending to become more of a holiday centre than a hydrotherapy centre. In 1919, however, it was still in active practice, so to speak, Dr T. D. Luke's *Spas and Health Resorts of The British Isles*, published in that year, noting that, 'There are considerable facilities in the way of baths at Malvern, although no actual pump room and central bathing establishment,' and referring to 'the excellent hydropathic' which is said to be 'well equipped'. Today, however, for all practical purposes there is nothing left of hydrotherapy but St Anne's Well where the water can be drunk. There is still, however, the charm and beauty of the countryside, which, combined with what was described at the turn of the century as 'the dryness and equability of the climate and the gently stimulating character of the air', will for all time place the Malvern Hills high among the beauty spots of England.

As Malvern was being put on the hydrotherapy map of England, the other English convert from Grafenberg, Hamer Stansfield, a former mayor of Leeds, was staking his claim in Wharfedale, where, in 1846, a mile or so from Ilkley he opened the hydropathic establishment known as Ben Rhydding. Built at a cost of £30,000, it was variously known as the 'Northern Grafenberg' and the 'Yorkshire Malvern'. After a somewhat stock start under the medical control of an imported German hydrotherapist, it blossomed out under the aegis of Dr William Macleod, whose approach to hydrotherapy, it has been said, 'was nothing if not eclectic'. What one Victorian writer described as 'a peculiar feature' of his therapeutic regime was the compressed air bath, of which he was inordinately proud.

In the history of English hydrotherapy, however, Ben Rhydding's main claim to fame is its responsibility for converting John Smedley to a fanatical belief in hydrotherapy. Smedley was a North Derbyshire textile manufacturer who decided in his late 30s that the time had come to enjoy his hard-earned profits, a process which involved the traditional Grand Tour of Europe. Coming back from this in a rather worse state than he set out, he was persuaded to take the cure at Ben Rhydding. Here, according to one commentator, 'aided by a mixture of cold sheets and wet douches', he underwent 'not only a conversion to hydrotherapy but a spiritual conversion too'. Back at his mills in Matlock, the 'new man' applied the strict principles of hydrotherapy then practised at Ben Rhydding (Dr Macleod later modified them to attract more clients) to his employees. So successful were the results that he decided that it was his duty to make them available to all and sundry – at a price – and in the 1850s he opened the Smedley Hydropathic in Matlock. In a short time, such was his success, he had more than two thousand clients a year and had to extend his premises. Ten years later, having made a second fortune out of hydrotherapy, he built himself Riber Castle, in which he spent the rest of his life in considerable style. Today Smedley's Hydro houses the offices of what was the Derbyshire County Council and the grounds of the semi-ruined Riber Castle have been converted into a zoo. Matlock's reputation as a hydropathic centre, however, persisted, attracting many rivals to Smedley's Hydro, and even as late as 1919 it was reported that there were between thirty and forty hydros, as they had then become known.

These two hydrotherapeutic 'money spinners' started a craze, or fashion, that spread throughout the length and breadth of the land. Interestingly enough, and for no apparent reason, the fashion caught on particularly in Scotland. Whether this was to compensate for the national lack of traditional spas, or whether it was a tribute to the financial acumen of the Scot, is an open question, but they undoubtedly proved a rich source of income throughout the late Victorian, Edwardian and Georgian periods.

Neither was Scotland slow off the mark, and it is perhaps only fitting that one of the first enthusiastic advocates of hydrotherapy north of the Tweed should have been an academic: Professor J. S. Blackie, the distinguished classical scholar. In *The Water Cure in Scotland* he gives a quite alarming picture of the effect of the water cure as he experienced it at Kirn. 'At Kirn, as at Grafenberg, people get drunk on pure water . . . Some of us about the end of the fourth week or so, get rid of our superfluous store of nervous energy, become pugilistic and fall to buffeting our neighbours . . . while two-thirds spout copious blank verse from the close mummy-bandage of the wet sheet and jingle hydrotherapeutic rhymes beneath the douche.' An example of *joie de vivre* scarcely compatible with the traditional solemnity of the Scottish dominie, and a striking contrast to the already quoted comments of Carlyle on the Malvern hydrotherapeutic regime.

A typical example of the Scottish hydropathics of the period was that at Bridge of Allan on Robert Burns' romantic Allan Water near Stirling. So well known did it become that it was known as the 'Scottish Grafenberg'. Presumably Bridge of Allan was chosen for this purpose as its Airthrey Mineral Springs had been patronized from what a guide book of the mid-Victorian era describes as a 'very remote period', adding: 'A century back, the country folk were in the habit of flocking to the spot in fine weather and on Sundays for the purpose of receiving benefit from the waters,' and quoting a Dr Forrest of Stirling as claiming that, 'In their amount of saline impregnation' they were 'only inferior to some of the springs of Cheltenham and Leamington.' 'They are considered efficacious', it notes, 'in affections of the skin, stomach, and liver, in mild pulmonary symptoms, and in some cases of gout.'

The Strathearn Hydropathic Establishment at Crieff, neatly described in the 1865 edition of *Black's Picturesque Tourist of Scotland* as the 'second largest village in Perthshire next to Blairgowrie', and popularly known today as the 'Gateway to the Highlands', is typical of how these Scottish hydros developed. According to *The History of Crieff*, Dr Thomas H. Meikle, who owned a small hydro in Aberdeen, of which university he was a graduate, 'considered it advisable to find a more central spot than Aberdeen, and after examining various localities in Scotland in 1866, expressed himself as thoroughly satisfied with the bracing climate of Strathearn.' Another possible explanation for this choice is that a few years earlier mineral wells had been discovered in the neighbourhood of Crieff which, on analysis, had proved to be saline in character, and the local laird had made them available in a 'rustic well-house'. Whatever his reasons, Dr Meikle founded a company in 1867, with a capital of £25,000 in 840 shares, which, it is interesting to note, were almost immediately fully subscribed. A site of around 15 acres was bought and a hydropathic was built at a cost of £30,000, described in a contemporary guide book as 'a large and elegant building which is provided with every appliance of hydrotherapy'. When it opened in 1868 it originally used the water from the mineral springs but later this was supplemented with water from Loch Turrett when this was laid on as the piped source of water for Crieff. For many years it was a popular convalescent centre for the ailing Scottish clergy who were offered special reduced terms out of season.

Medicinal wells, however, were by no means a *sine qua non* in choosing a site for a Scottish hydropathic establishment. The expansion of the railways was making the holiday attractions of

Scotland more accessible, and clearly the enterprising Scot felt that a combination of scenery and hydrotherapy was a sound one. Thus was established in 1878 the Hotel Hydro at Peebles in the valley of the Tweed. The original building was destroyed by fire in 1905 but rebuilt on an even more elaborate scale, and in 1919 was described as having 'an almost unique position among establishments of this nature in Great Britain, having an elaborate equipment of baths and everything that is associated with a complete modern spa.' Alas, in 1977, although retaining the title of Hotel Hydro, and still possessing all the advantages of a beautifully sited hotel in a lovely stretch of country, all that is left of the 'Hydro' are sauna baths, massage, 'electrical treatment', and a swimming pool.

'The old order changeth, yielding place to new,' as Tennyson noted, and perhaps in this age of increasing specialization it became unavoidable that the two functions of a hydro and a hotel had to be separated. While not incompatible they require two distinct skills. A further factor is the extent to which the hotel habit has spread throughout the community, and an almost inevitable corollary to this is that the modern healthy holidaymaker does not wish to find himself in a hotel with a large quota of the ailing undergoing treatment. This is where the spa scores. With its patients scattered throughout a range of hotels and boarding houses, undergoing treatment under skilled supervision, it allows its hotels to concentrate on their main task of providing comfortable accommodation, efficient service and an attractive menu suitable for the relaxed and restful mode of life which is an integral part of spas that heal.

15

Continental spas

While the powers that be wipe the map of Britain clean of spas, continental spas are booming. Outside Scandinavia and The Netherlands there is not a European country on either side of the Iron Curtain that has not its spas, and in every case they have the enthusiastic backing of the medical profession. Granted that in some instances the term is used rather loosely – more in the sense of what we would call a health resort – but in the vast majority of cases they provide the traditional mixture of medicinal waters, used internally and/or externally, rest and relaxation. A brief glance at a representative sample of these continental spas that heal will demonstrate their scope and the high estimation in which they are held by the doctors of the countries concerned.

Austria

Austria has 108 spas. These are controlled by Government regulations which are applied by individual provinces and lay down minimal requirements of quality. Therapeutic agents must be natural and possess scientifically recognized therapeutic effects, and for this purpose a certificate must be issued by the Federal

Institute for Experimental Pharmacological and Balneological Examination of Vienna. In addition, provincial governments check the standards and hygiene of the spa buildings and equipment, and the water is submitted to control analysis every five years. Indeed, it is claimed that 'In no other country do such strict regulations for the protection of spa patients exist.'

Be that as it may, and in spite of the poetic licence that some of the spas allow themselves in advertising their waters, there is no doubt that the over-all standards of Austrian spas are commendably high. This was certainly the impression I gathered from the three I have visited. Typical of these was that at Baden bei Wien, nestling in the Vienna Woods some 16 miles from the capital, and a popular resort of Beethoven. With a history going back some two thousand years, its fifteen springs produce water at a temperature of around 36° C. (97° F.), containing calcium, sodium, sulphate and chloride as well as sulphur. The Spa Treatment Centre is modern and up to date in its equipment, and provides a wide range of treatment, particularly for rheumatic diseases.

The Austrian spas include over twenty Kneipp hydrotherapy centres which practise the form of hydrotherapy introduced by Pastor Sebastian Kneipp of Worshofen last century, as described in chapter 14. Basically this consists of alternating cold applications with hot partial baths and packs, combined with a dietary regime (largely vegetarian) and regular walks. It is a modified form of hydrotherapy which has retained its popularity in the German-speaking countries, and undoubtedly seems to suit the Teutonic temperament.

While the Austrian spas, like their opposite numbers in other countries, go all out to attract foreign visitors of whom they attract a steady stream year after year, the bulk of their patients are Austrians, many of whom receive their treatment under the aegis of Krankenhassa, the Austrian National Health Service.

Czechoslovakia

Czechoslovakia is particularly well organized in the spa world. As one commentator, writing in 1963, put it: 'Although Czechoslovakia has an area of only 127,800 square kilometres, there are about one hundred well-equipped health resorts and an equal number of thermal and mineral springs with some modest equipment and mostly used by the inhabitants of the region.' The best known of these, of course, are Carlsbad (or Karlovy Vary as it is now known), Marienbad (or Marianski Lazne) and Piestany.

Carlsbad, founded by and named by the Emperor Charles IV in 1347, had its social hey-day, like Bath, in the eighteenth and nineteenth centuries, but it still retains much of its old-world charm. Its waters are bottled and Karlovy Vary salt is exported for medical use in reconstituted form. Marienbad, beloved of King Edward VII, and recently achieving vicarious fame as the result of a justifiably popular film, specializes in the drinking of the waters from its thirty-eight springs, and the treatment of obesity. Piestany, on the other hand, is famous for its mud packs and stakes its claim to therapeutic fame by incorporating in its coat of arms a man breaking and throwing away his crutches. While, like many of the other spas in the country, foreign visitors are catered for, full use is made of all of them for the treatment of those citizens of the country who require spa therapy.

France

With 1200 mineral springs, France claims to be 'one of the richest countries in medical water resources'. It is also one of the best organized, with legislation dating back to 1823. Under this legislation the commercial exploitation of a natural mineral spring is subject to prior authorization by the Ministry of Social Affairs. Once this licence has been granted, the spring can be scheduled as of public interest by the Conseil d'Etat. The subsequent exploitation of such mineral springs is subject to a double control: technical supervision by the Mining Service for all matters affecting preservation and development, and hygiene supervision by the health authorities, including the National Public Health Laboratory and the Service of Thermalism and General Water Hygiene. Control of the one hundred French spas, including the treatment provided, is in the hands of the National Syndicate of Thermal Establishments. All organizations concerned with the exploitation of mineral springs are grouped into the French Thermal and Climatic Federation, which co-ordinates their activities.

In addition, according to a bulletin issued by the French Embassy, 'Doctors are also required to have scientific knowledge of the various spas, their physical, chemical and biological characteristics and the complaints for which they offer specialized treatment. All these matters are taught in the departments of hydro-climatology of the universities, as part of the medical curricula. In varying degrees, factors such as the size of spas, the quality of treatment facilities, the properties of the waters, etc., are all relevant to the doctor's decision to recommend one spa rather than another in each specific case.

'Knowledge in this field is being constantly increased in a great number of laboratories and specialized institutes, which carry on research on the spot. Outside the spas, several universities possess institutes of hydrology and climatology, in particular those of Paris, Clermont-Ferrand and Toulouse.

'For instance, the Paris Institute of Hydrology and Climatology has Analytical Chemistry and Hydrology Services whose laboratories analyse mineral waters, contribute to the development of new methods of analysis, to the study of the origin, composition, general properties and classification of waters, as well as to the prospection and study of soils and the planning and general technology of cure establishments. The same Institute's Services of Biochemistry and Physiology applied to Hydrology and Climatology carry on research into the ways in which mineral

Aix-les-Bains. The thermal establishment and the Grand Hotel. In the foreground are the remains of a Roman arch. *French Government Tourist Office.*

waters act and into the physiological and therapeutic properties of cures.'

'This', it adds, 'explains why a patient can take a water-cure on Social Security, for one of the chief objects of the French Social Security System is to enable the insured to undergo all suitable therapeutic treatments. Since a water-cure involves other expenses besides those of actual treatment (transport, accommodation), which patients cannot always afford, the following principle has been adopted: the fees of the doctors following the progress of the cure on the spot and the cost of treatment at the thermal establishment are covered by sickness insurance in all cases where the need for a water-cure is recognized; while the transport and accommodation expenses of the patient and, in justifiable cases, of the accompanying person, are reimbursed only if his means are inadequate.

'Furthermore, under the terms of provisions in force in the European Economic Community since 1 July 1968, patients from Common Market countries can claim Social Security benefits for water-cures in any of the member countries.'

As a result, today Social Security patients account for practically three-quarters of those going to spas. According to the Union des Caisses Nationales de Sécurité Sociale, 319,073 French patients took the cure at French spas in 1974. A further interesting indication of the extent to which French spas are coming under state control is the fact that five spa establishments, including those at Aix-les-Bains, Plombières and Vichy, belong to the State. The National Baths of Aix-les-Bains are the only ones organized as a public administrative establishment enjoying (if that is the right word) legal status and financial autonomy. The others are run by private enterprise, the State being represented in each by a Government commissioner.

Germany

In West Germany spas are big business. In 1972, spa treatment cost the nation around 10,000 million marks, which corresponds to 2 per cent of the Federal Republic's gross national product. In view of these figures, which certainly have not decreased in the last six years, it is scarcely surprising that one commentator has noted that, 'It is understandable that the public, and particularly the medical profession, are increasingly worried as to whether these large investments are really meaningful – and above all, successful.'

The resultant strain on the German Pension Insurance Fund was enhanced, it would appear, by a tendency for at least a certain section of the German profession to prescribe spa therapy indiscriminately, with the result that all too many patients were sent to what were often attractive holiday resorts without adequate medical reason and without even taking the prescribed course of treatment, or 'Cure' as it is traditionally known in Germany. This, it should be added, is a phenomenon by no means confined to German doctors and patients.

In spite of this partial abuse of spa therapy and national insurance funds, a report based on a ten-year follow-up study of 7000 members of the Pension Insurance Fund showed a drop of around two-thirds in the duration of the illness and the cost of treatment following spa therapy. 'In spite of all the disparaging remarks about balneotherapy', it is noted, 'and the claims that it had become obsolete, the long-term effects were extremely favourable.' In addition, attention is drawn to the fact that, 'The decline in absenteeism and the fall in treatment costs also included an improvement of the patients' state of health, and that is what counts primarily.'

These German doubts about the value of spa therapy have been deliberately quoted in some detail as they so resemble those expressed in Britain. Any state-subsidized form of treatment is bound to be abused, but it seems clear that the German authorities are satisfied as to the benefits accruing from spas that heal.

Altogether, 280 spas are listed in the current handbook of the German Spa Association, of which around 200 are spas in the conventional sense of the term. The others include Kneipp resorts and even seaside resorts. All these spas are under strict Government control, and quite a complicated procedure has to be gone through before a spa is officially recognized. In 1975, 6,150,000 Germans visited these spas, spending an average of 11·9 days there. In addition there were 469,000 foreign visitors who spent an average of 3·5 days. From this last figure it is clear that it was only a proportion of these foreign visitors who took the cure. Indeed, the average for the German visitors indicates that only some of them could have taken a prescribed course of treatment, as this is never less than two weeks.

Nevertheless, there is no evidence of the Germans losing faith in their spas. Thus, at Baden-Baden 24 new hotels are planned in the medium price range, partly to tempt visitors to stay for longer periods of treatment. In 1976, Baden-Baden had 800,000 visitors, about half of whom came for spa therapy. Between them they provided the casino, reported to be the wealthiest in the world, with an income of DM34m., 80 per cent of which was paid in tax to the Land government, with a large proportion of this being returned to the town.

These spa facilities are basically available to all German citizens under their equivalent of our National Health Service. In severe cases the appropriate Pension Insurance Fund will foot the bill. In all other cases it will refund a certain proportion. As a rule this is of little significance as most Germans subscribe also to supplementary private insurance schemes (*Ersatzkasse*) which pay the difference between the National Insurance contribution and the actual cost. The usual procedure is that the patient's doctor recommends the treatment, the National Insurance authorities and the private insurance authorities check this, and, as a rule, the patient is examined by a consultant physician before a final decision is reached as to whether spa therapy is indicated.

Hungary

Hungary is the home of hot springs. More than 500 (123 in Budapest alone) gush forth 430,000 litres of water, above 35° C. (95° F.) in temperature, every minute. Of this never-ending supply of hot water, around 40 per cent is used for medicinal purposes. The remainder is used for heating the new blocks of flats going up in Budapest, for greenhouses and for supplementing the drinking-water supplies in areas of the country with inadequate cold-water supplies. The daily output from the 123 springs in Budapest is 40 million litres of hot water and 30 million litres of lukewarm water. The hottest of the springs yields water at 74° C. (165° F.). Their composition ranges from 1 gram per litre of dis-

The Thermal Hotel, Heviz, Hungary. Opened in 1976, the hotel has 217 single and double bedrooms, a swimming pool filled with water from the thermal lake, a sauna and a solarium. Medical examinations take place in the hotel.

solved substances to waters containing calcium, magnesium, sodium sulphate, radon and hydrogen sulphide – in varying amounts.

To ensure the optimal utilization of this abundance of thermal springs, the National Institute for Rheumatology and Physiotherapy in Budapest carries out continuing research into the physical and chemical properties of the water from different springs, their mode of action and their optimal method of administration, as well as other current problems in the treatment of rheumatic diseases.

Both in Budapest, where there are eight spas (or treatment centres), and outside the capital, hospitals or spas have been built at the site of tried and tested hot springs. Here the natural resources are combined with the services of a fully-qualified medical staff. Perhaps the best-known of these is at Heviz where a natural hot-water lake is fed by thermal springs.

Known since Roman times, people have travelled to Heviz for centuries to bathe in this lake, 12 acres in area and with its water completely exchanged every other day as it is replenished from a hot spring, the average yield of which is 36,000 litres a minute. During the summer the temperature of the water runs around 33° to 35° C. (91° to 95° F.), and even in winter it does not fall below 26° C. (79° F.). A modern treatment centre was built in the 1960s which provides a wide range of treatment under a skilled residential staff of doctors and physiotherapists.

The Hungarians make full use of these thermal riches. In 1975, half a million Hungarians and foreign patients were treated in Hungarian spas. What proportion of these were foreigners is not known, but must have been relatively small. Spa therapy is available free of charge to all Hungarians who require it. In addition, subsidized holidays are offered by trade unions to their members, 75 per cent of the cost being shared by the union and the State. These holidays, of two to three weeks' duration, are usually at spas where hostels are provided at which the trade unionists stay with their families. Here they may relax or have any of the spa therapy that the doctors consider would be beneficial.

Italy

Italy is the home of mud packs, but its spas offer a wide variety of spa therapy. As an Italian commentator has said, 'Medical hydrology in Italy dates to the prehistory of medicine, when ablution at springs assumed a special significance more ritual than therapeutic.' Today, however, an increasingly rational and scientific approach is being made to the subject, and there are now several chairs of medical hydrology in Italian universities, which constitutes an integral part of the medical curriculum.

As in the case of Poland and the U.S.S.R., precise figures are difficult to come by in Italy but, according to the director of one Italian spa, writing in 1963, 'The continuing development of spa therapy in Italy has led to widespread acceptance by the people.' At that time, 'About 20 per cent of patients receiving treatment at spas were supported there by third-party payments.' Writing in the current edition of *Thermal Baths in Italy*, issued by the Italian State Tourist Office, Professor Mariano Messini, Professor of Systematic Medical Therapy and Medical Hydrology in the University of Rome, reports that, 'Since the end of World War II, five times as many foreign and Italian patients are taking the cure in our spas.' 'This indicates', he adds, 'widespread and growing recognition of the great efficacy of natural treatment, of which that provided by the spas dealt with in this volume is an excellent example.' In 1960, the latest year for which I have been able to obtain figures, more than a million patients received 15 million treatments at Italian spas. So, obviously, business is booming and the Italian medical profession and their patients are satisfied that there are spas that heal.

In spite of its trace of chauvinism, it is probably not remiss to conclude this short review of spa therapy in Italy with a further quotation from Professor Messini. 'Spa treatment is used to achieve three fundamental aims of medicine: prevention; treatment of morbid conditions in the case of some illnesses and of convalescent conditions in others, assisting complete recovery; and of rehabilitation. The ancient traditions are followed in a larger number of spas in Italy than elsewhere, but another remarkable feature is the scientific study of the mechanism by which mineral waters act through drinking, mud, inhalation, irrigation and other techniques, with the aim of establishing the exactly appropriate treatment for each complaint. I make this statement in my capacity as chairman of the Permanent Committee of the International Society of Medical Hydrology and of the Medinische

Komission of the Internationale Vereinigung fur Balneologie-Klimatologie.'

Israel

As a supplement – not a postscript – to this chapter, a brief note may be appended on current developments of what the Israeli Health Research Authority describes as 'the Dead Sea as an International Spa Resort'. 'The Dead Sea and the thermal springs in its immediate vicinity', it is claimed, 'have all the potentialities for turning the area into one of the most important spa regions in the world.' Accordingly, a stretch of the west coast is 'being planned as a spa of international standard so that it will be able to cater to all who will want to come "to take the cure" in the Dead Sea and the nearby hot springs'.

The current medical interest in this development is the claim that is being made for the benefit produced in psoriasis by bathing in the Dead Sea. Since 1971, large numbers of Danish victims of this distressing disease have been undergoing such treatment under the aegis of the Danish National Health Service and, according to a report by two Copenhagen doctors, at the end of a two-year programme involving the treatment of 600 patients with psoriasis, over 90 per cent were 'either improved or the skin completely recovered'.

This is not the place to discuss the risks involved in claiming 'complete recovery' in psoriasis, as every victim of the disease knows to his cost, but these results, if confirmed, do suggest that there may be something in this combined therapy of Dead Sea baths, rest and sunshine. These preliminary results are not reported here to raise false hopes. Indeed, a firm warning must be interpolated that no patient with psoriasis should dream of undertaking this treatment without consulting his doctor.

What is significant, and possibly of practical therapeutic value, is that here is a fresh development in the healing potentialities of spas. And, as one visitor to the Ein Bohek Spa, where the treatment is carried out, has commented, the Holy Bible records more than one individual being cured of his skin disease by bathing in these waters. How many of them were suffering from psoriasis we know not, but it is an interesting thought that modern Israel may have rediscovered an old form of treatment known to their ancestors and recorded in the Old Testament.

16

The rationale of spas

'If mineral waters be actually in themselves, physiologically and medicinally speaking, powerful remedies in the cure of disease, their beneficial effects are assisted in most cases by every adjuvant that can render the remedy one taken under favourable circumstances. In the case of these remedies the practitioner and the patient meet on common ground. Every man of sense and education can judge of the benefits of pure air, abstraction from business and care, and to a certain extent of the amount of benefit derived from hot and cold baths; and the patient who frequents mineral waters is pretty sure to ask himself the question, how much of the benefit he may derive is to be ascribed to hygienic conditions, how much to the actual potency of the remedy in the mineral water? In this way, perhaps, if his mind be of an inquisitive turn, he may be led to consideration of questions vital to medicine – viz, how far drugs are beneficial? how far they may be abused?

'. . . When we consider the vast number of conditions which, in the case of recoveries from the use of a mineral water, may concur in the production of the beneficial result, it is easy to see how arduous a task it must be to assign those conditions which contribute more than others to this result. The more important is it, then, that medical men should have, if possible, fixed principles with regard to the use of these remedies, principles to which they may refer as guides amid so many conflicting statements and opinions.'

This quotation, taken from the *British and Foreign Medico-Chirurgical Review* of 1857, has a triple interest and justification for use as the introduction to this chapter. In the first place it illustrates that 'inquisitive' patients are no innovation of the present day. They existed a hundred and twenty years ago, and not only existed but were tolerated by at least a section of the medical profession of those days. There may not have been a Patients' Association then, but the makings of one existed. On the other hand, one wonders whether perhaps such an organized association was entirely unnecessary in those days because doctors were able to devote time to individual patients to answer all their questions – or at least satisfy them that their cases were being carefully considered in all their aspects.

In the second place it shows, or at least suggests, that questions were raised as to the benefits of drugs and their abuses. Equally significant is the fact that the double possibility – of the ineffective use and the misuse of drugs – is raised in such a matter-of-fact way, without apparent metaphorical raising of medical eyebrows but rather as a routine problem that should be taken into consideration.

Thirdly, and most important of all from the point of view of the thesis of this chapter, it shows that the precise rationale of spa therapy was not understood. Equally important, it emphasizes that such therapy is anything but a single, simple formula. Rather is it a form of combined therapy of such intricacy that it is difficult to ascribe its benefits to one part of it rather than another.

The twelve decades that have elapsed have clarified some points, but thrown little light on others. What the passage of time has made abundantly clear is that the unique feature of a spa is the way in which it combines physical and psychological factors. It treats the whole patient, not just his disease. It encourages a rapport between the patient on the one hand, and the doctor and physiotherapist on the other. This takes place ideally in an atmosphere far removed from the 'madding crowd' and the stress of and strains of everyday life – whether these be those of the office or the home. This is why it is so important that a spa should be an attractive town, township, village, call it what you may, in attractive surroundings where the patient can relax, enjoy good food, good company, good music and lovely countryside. In such surroundings he can relax psychologically as well as physically and mentally, and thereby derive full benefit from all the ancillary forms of treatment to which he is submitted.

This is why the ideal is an initial course of treatment of at least two weeks, longer if possible. In the case of chronic conditions – and it is for the chronic ailments of life that spas are best adapted – such a course of treatment should be repeated annually, or at least every other year. In between the visits to a spa, the patient can continue with his treatment on an outpatient basis at his local home hospital. But no hospital, no matter how efficient its hydrotherapy department, massage, physical medicine, or rheumatic department, whatever it may be named, is a complete and effective substitute for a spa.

On the physical side, the primary form of treatment is the use of the waters of the spa. These may be taken internally, or in the form of baths and the like. It is this latter use, or hydrotherapy as it is known, that constitutes the greater part of spa treatment today but, before discussing this, brief reference must be made to their internal use.

This is not the place to go into a detailed classification of the various forms of waters available at different spas. So far as British spas are concerned little significance is attached to the drinking of the waters. Even on the continent, decreasing attention is being devoted to this form of spa therapy, except at a few spas such as Carlsbad, Marienbad, Spa, Vichy and Vittel. The chief conditions for which they are used can be grouped into two main lots: various forms of dyspepsia (apart from gastric and duodenal ulcers), liver and gall-bladder disease; and stones in the kidneys and bladder.

In the case of the former, two main groups of waters are used: those which have a soothing effect on the disordered gut, and those which have a laxative action. Precisely how beneficial this is, is arguable. It may well be that the benefit, which undoubtedly accrues in many cases, is the result of the orderly, restful regime that the patient is following. On the other hand, as so often in medicine, one must not be too dogmatic – as is illustrated by a theory at present circulating in medical circles.

This concerns Epsom salts, or magnesium sulphate – so classified geographically because it was the active constituent of the waters which made Epsom one of the best-known spas in England in the seventeenth century. It is a potent laxative and its popularity has continued ever since. Indeed, it was one of the first cut-price drugs that Jesse Boot put on display in his original herbal shop in Goose Street, Nottingham. Epsom was by no means the only spa whose waters contained magnesium salts, including the sulphate, and the laxative, or purgative, action of them is largely due to the magnesium sulphate they contain. Evidence is now forthcoming that a certain number of fatal cases of coronary heart disease may be due to a deficiency of magnesium. It is certainly known that magnesium is essential for the normal functioning of the heart, and the heart has the highest concentration of magnesium of any organ in the body. There is also quite impressive evidence that the heart muscle of patients dying suddenly of coronary heart disease contains significantly smaller concentrations of magnesium than heart muscle from patients dying of other diseases.

Whether this is a true bill is not yet known, but it certainly suggests that, particularly in middle age and onwards, a regular intake of a magnesium salt, not necessarily Epsom salts, may not only do no harm, but may even be beneficial. If this should be so, then our medical forebears who advised their patients to drink the magnesium-containing waters at their favourite spa may have been wiser than they realized. Or, in the words of a contributor to *The Lancet*, 'The saying, "enough to cover a sixpence", may be even wiser than we thought.'

The rationale of the drinking of mineral waters in the treatment of stone in the kidneys and bladder is primarily the simple plumbing one of flushing out the 'gravel' from which the stones are formed. This does not necessarily guarantee that stones will not form, but it certainly reduces the risk. Such stones, or calculi as they are technically known, are not nearly as common in western countries as they used to be, but they still occur and, in spite of much intensive, high-powered research, there is no known antidote to them – either in the form of a preventive or a drug that will dissolve them once they are formed and before they have attained a size sufficient to demand surgical removal.

In addition, altering the reaction of the urine from acid to alkaline, or vice-versa, depending upon the type of stone that is present, may be helpful, and here again the drinking of spa waters may be of use. At one time this principle of producing a diuresis – or an ample flow of urine in lay terms – was also of value in treating infections of the kidneys and bladder, particularly the latter (the condition known as cystitis). Indeed, up until the discovery of the sulphonamides (or sulpha drugs), and later antibiotics, this was a widely used method of treating such infections.

The external use of water as a means of treatment, or hydrotherapy, is one of the oldest forms of therapy. As Dr Simon Baruch, the G.O.M. of United States hydrotherapy, pointed out, 'Of all remedial agents in use since the dawn of medicine, water is the only one that has survived all the vicissitudes of doctrinal changes.' To which he added: 'No remedial agent merits the confidence of the physician unless it fulfils the following conditions: (a) Ready accessibility; (b) a rationale ascertained by experiments on a physiological basis; (c) facility of dosage; (d) reliable clinical observations. Water meets these demands. Water is not only readily accessible, but it may be used in the liquid, solid, and vaporized form, each of which has its therapeutic value.'

Writing in 1920, he supplements this with a comment which has a suspiciously topical ring: 'During the past few decades pharmacy has advanced greatly, not in the development of curative agents, but in palliatives for relieving pain and reducing temperature, etc., the too active use of which interferes with the conservative process of nature. Today we are overwhelmed by a new polypharmacy of drugs sold in ready-made packages that contributes more to the comfort of the doctor than to the safety of the patient. That water, which has survived all vicissitudes, still is forced to struggle for existence is due to the neglect of physicians, if we may judge from its non-use despite reliable facts above stated. The day will surely come when physicians will return to the saner practice.' His final testament at the end of a long life of service to medicine was that he had never regarded water as otherwise than a rational aid to the *vis medicatrix naturae*.

In this belief he was in a great medical tradition stretching from Thales of Miletus (639–544 B.C.), the Greek philosopher who is credited with foretelling an eclipse of the sun and introducing geometry into Greece and who held that water is the ultimate essence of all things, through Hippocrates, known for two millennia as the Father of Medicine, who used hydrotherapy with and without massage for the treatment of muscle and joint disease, and Galen, the leading physician of the Roman era who gave water first place in the treatment of disease, to the present day. Nor in this great tradition must the name of John Wesley be overlooked. His *Primitive Physic*, first published in 1747, and reprinted many times, may have been frowned upon by contemporary orthodox physicians, but it is crammed full of sound practical advice, with persistent emphasis on the benefits of hydrotherapy (as we now call it), exercise and diet. Typical of his aphorisms are:

'Cold-bathing is of great advantage to health; it prevents abundance of diseases; it promotes perspiration, helps the circulation of the blood, and prevents the danger of catching cold.'

John Wesley. *From a painting after Romney. National Portrait Gallery, London.*

For gout: 'At six in the evening, undress and wrap yourself up in blankets. Then put your legs up to the knees in water, as hot as you can bear it. As it cools, let hot water be poured in, so as to keep you in a strong sweat till ten. Then go to bed well warmed and sweat till morning – I have known this cure an inveterate gout, in a person above sixty, who lived eleven years after.'

For 'the rheumatism': 'Use the cold bath with rubbing or sweating; or apply warm steams.'

For sciatica: 'Use cold bathing, and sweat, together with the flesh-brush twice a day.'

For 'a white swelling' (on the joints): 'Hold the foot half an hour every morning, under a pump or cock. This cures also all pains in joints. It seldom fails; tried. Or a stream of cold water one day, and warm the next, and so on by turns.'

This fascinating book, which should be compulsory reading for every young doctor, and every self-styled health educator, whether Government subsidized or not, concludes with an appendix listing the conditions for which cold-bathing is indicated. This ends with two interesting paragraphs:

'Wise parents should dip their children in cold water every morning, till they are three quarters old; and afterwards their hands and feet'.

'Washing the head every morning in cold water, prevents rheums, and cures coughs, old head-aches [e.g., the morning after the night before?], and sore eyes.'

Before leaving Wesley, the wise, if unqualified family physician, a passing reference must be made to his treatment for 'raging madness': 'Apply to the head cloths dipt in cold water; or, set the patient with his head under a great water-fall, as long as his strength will bear; or pour water on his head out of a kettle.' This was one of the more humane forms of treatment for maniacal patients, and it was one that was practised well into the present century. A standard textbook, *Hydrotherapy*, published in the

U.S.A. in 1910, contains an entire section devoted to 'Insanity'. A somewhat primitive, if safe, form of 'shock therapy' recommended, the converse of Wesley's, was the use of continuous warm baths for cases of 'moderate excitement'. An interesting testimonial to the efficacy of hydrotherapy in mental illness is that of one Massachusetts patient who had had delusions of demoniacal possession: 'Your baths are excellent to reduce cerebral excitement. You can't fight the devil with fire, he is in his element there, but he is mortally afraid of cold water.'

Modern psychiatrists may frown on the use of hydrotherapy in the treatment of mental illness, but in the physical sphere it is still one of our great standbys in the treatment of certain forms of disease, and might be described as the king-pin of spa therapy. Its value depends upon mechanical and therapeutic effects.

When a body is immersed in water it is acted upon, according to the principle of Archimedes, by an upward vertical force equal to the weight of water displaced. This means that a patient entering a bath will be supported to a great extent by the surrounding water. In other words, body weight and, incidentally, friction, are eliminated. The practical significance of this has been admirably summarized by an experienced physiotherapist: 'In the fulness of time the animal world evolved man, with his mastery of the technique of highly co-ordinated movements while balanced on a very small base. When reconditioning this highly complex piece of machinery it is advantageous to employ a medium which temporarily relieves it of the combat against gravity, while we build up its resources.'

In practice what this means is that any movement to raise a limb to a higher level is aided by the buoyancy of the water but, when the limb is lowered, this buoyancy acts as a resisting force. Thus the buoyancy of the water can be used to assist or resist muscle action, and active movements can be performed which weak muscles are unable to achieve without this help. Warm, relaxed, and unhindered by clothes, the crippled patient, whatever the cause, can move his limbs, provided the paralysis is not complete, and gradually regain the optimum range of movement compatible with his disease. The patient may not be able to take up his bed and walk, but he will regain a certain degree of mobility, and as often as not this means that, in modern medical jargon, he becomes ambulant and is able to get about under his own steam. If the buoyancy of the water is increased, as in the brine baths at Droitwich, then the effect is even more beneficial.

The temperature of the water has an equally useful effect. If it is warm, this produces dilatation of the blood vessels, which is beneficial to the function of weak or spastic muscles. This vasodilatation, as it is known, not only helps the wasted muscles associated with painful joint conditions, but also helps to relieve the pain which is often a dominating factor limiting the amount of movement in a joint. Thus, with relief of pain the joint can move more freely, especially if the buoyancy of the water assists the movement of the muscles. In this way, as it has been aptly summarized, 'The treatment overcomes the vicious circle of a painful stiff joint leading to disuse muscle atrophy, a weak atrophied muscle trying ineffectively to move a stiff joint and the joint thus becoming stiffer and the muscle weaker.'

All sorts of variations can be played on this theme: cold baths; partial baths in which, for example, only a limb is immersed; douches and sprays of various forms and contrast baths, in which limbs are immersed in hot and cold baths alternately.

Hot and cold packs are also used. Of these the best known are mud packs, or pelotherapy as it is technically known. Peloid, according to the International Society of Medical Hydrology, is the generic name for substances that originate in nature by geological processes and, in a finely divided state mixed with water, are applied to baths and packs in medical practice. There is a wide range of substances included in this definition, including mud from various sources and peat. In some cases they are of mineral origin, as in many of the Italian muds known as fango, the Italian for mud. In other cases, such as those of marine or estuary origin, they contain much organic matter, whilst in others, as in that obtained from the bottom of the thermal lake at Heviz, the well-known Hungarian spa, they contain a wide variety of mineral and organic matter.

Opinion is divided as to their mode of action. 'Some', it has been said, 'believe that it is physical; others, chemical; and still others, physiochemical.' Whatever other action they may have, they hold heat for a long time on account of their high specific heat and low heat conductivity, and therefore are a useful method of applying heat – either in the form of a bath or by application to localized parts of the body, such as the elbow or knee. In other words, as it has been expressed: 'The peloid may also be applied to appropriate areas, either limbs or trunk, in which case the application is very similar to a large kaolin poultice and indeed, kaolin being a clay, the action is similar.' Or, in the more homely language of a physiotherapist: 'Peat and such old friends as linseed and mustard are also used.' Another substitute for 'natural' peloids is fuller's earth. At Leamington Spa, 'mud packs' are prepared from fuller's earth bought from a local pharmacy.

New evidence, however, suggests that there may be more to peat packs at least. According to a report in *Nature*, the internationally recognized senior British scientific journal, of the fifth International Peat Congress in Poland in September 1976, 'One interesting aspect of the congress was the claim made for peat or peat preparations as a source of antiviral compounds, and of their use in the treatment of cancers, osteoarthrosis, and conditions arising from bronchial asthma.' The relevant section of the report, incidentally entitled 'Miraculous Peat?', so far as spa therapy is concerned reads as follows: 'In much of Europe, unlike Britain, spas, peat baths and indeed the general study of balneology are still very much a feature of the medical scene, and K. Weber and G. Plötner of the German Democratic Republic presented the results of various peat bath therapies in the treatment of rheumatoid arthritis. They concluded that whatever peat consistency they used, all their patients benefited by a reduction in their erythrocyte sedimentation rate.'

The erythrocyte sedimentation rate is one of the crucial laboratory tests used in the diagnosis of rheumatoid arthritis, in assessing its severity, and in determining its response to treatment. Compared with the patients' subjective reaction to treatment – for example, whether they feel less pain from the affected joints – it provides an objective, or scientific, gauge of the effect of treatment on the cause of the disease. If this East German report, and the other reports presented at this conference, are confirmed, a new and interesting phase will open up in the treatment of rheumatic diseases, incidentally confirming the claims that have been made for many a long year for the value of 'pelotherapy' as an essential constituent of therapy in the majority of spas.

Before passing to a brief consideration of other aspects of spa therapy, this is obviously the place to interpolate a note on one of the fundamental criticisms – indeed the only relevant one – advanced by a certain section of the medical profession, mainly rheumatologists, of spas. This is that the benefits of hydrotherapy can be obtained just as effectively in a hospital department as in a spa, because there is no special virtue in spa waters as compared with tap water.

The brief answer to this – and it can only be brief in a book such as this as it is such a complex technical problem – is that there is evidence that the constituents of the water in which patients are treated in spas do have a beneficial action compared with ordinary water. Modern medical research has shown how dependent we are for health, and indeed life, on what is known as the electrolyte balance of the body, or what Claude Bernard, the great French physiologist, over a hundred years ago described as the *milieu intérieur*. In many ways it is on a 'razor edge', to use Somerset Maugham's phrase, of balanced electrolytes – sodium, potassium, calcium, magnesium and the like – that the normal healthy functioning of the body is based. This balance can be affected not only by the many powerful drugs we now take by mouth, but also by absorption through the skin. Further, the effect of different waters, notably those containing carbon dioxide in natural solution, on the skin, and thus reflexly on, for example, the circulation and the nervous system, can be quite considerable.

Granted that the evidence in favour of this thesis is not one hundred per cent proven, and that it is not based on the carefully controlled clinical trials that the medical statisticians of today are so insistent upon. Conversely, and equally valid, is the contention that the critics of spas have not produced the scientific evidence proving its lack of efficacy, which doctors are fully justified in demanding before they discard a form of treatment that has persisted all down the ages. Until such condemnatory evidence is forthcoming, spa therapy must be allowed to continue. This is a point that will be further developed in chapter 18.

And now to revert to the other constituents of spa therapy. These include massage, exercises, electrotherapy and occupational therapy. Massage, it has rightly been said, 'is one of the oldest forms of treatment in the practice of physiotherapy but nowadays, being a predominantly passive treatment, it is used less frequently. At a spa hand massage may be given under a needle spray of water, or else a hot high-pressure douche may be used to produce the same effect.' What is important is that massage should be active rather than passive, and combined with graduated exercises to ensure that the patient is taking full advantage of the improvement in his condition produced by the hydrotherapy he is undergoing.

This is a point that was admirably exemplified by Dame Albertine Winner in the Founders' Lecture she delivered before the Chartered Society of Physiotherapy in 1969.

> 'When I was a student your title, it is true, was the Chartered Society of Massage and Medical Gymnastics, and much of your work was indeed rubbing and applying various electrical devices to patients who lay happily basking in the warm and relaxing glow. I remember it well as a patient – the baths, prickly and soothing, the warm comforting lamp and then the strong gentle hands of the masseuse,

> smoothing out one's knotted muscles and leaving one stimulated and refreshed. It was the sheer passivity of it that was so pleasant for a lazy person like me. What incentive is there to get better when things as nice as this happen, as long as one is a patient?
>
> 'Alas for me and my fellow sybarites – times have changed. The patient now really has to work. Active exercises, group exercises, remedial gymnastics, exercises in the pool – no longer does the patient have all the fun. The roles are reversed and the patient now has every incentive to get better; to his surprise he finds himself enjoying all this work, trying out his returning function and competing with his fellow patients; above all learning how to live a normal life even if, in some cases, disabilities remain and have to be compensated for by skilfully exploited residual abilities.'

Finally, a further word must be added about the psychological aspect of spa therapy. This is perhaps best summed up in two quotations. The first is from one of our most experienced physiotherapists: 'The advantages of pool therapy are too well known to emphasize here, but not the least of them is the psychological one, particularly in the case of the severely disabled. In the hands of a competent physiotherapist, pool therapy is a pleasurable adventure, but it should be remembered that it is a stepping-stone and not an end in itself. Even though great muscle power can be built up (and indeed, given the appropriate case, this is done), water is not mankind's customary medium, and optimum rehabilitation usually requires progressive dry-land training.'

The other is again from Dame Albertine Winner's Founders' Lecture: 'I recall a patient with severe spastic paraplegia [i.e., paralysis of the lower limbs] from multiple sclerosis and a strong hysterical overlay, and a physiotherapist, struggling with the spasm, saying to a psychotherapist, "I want you to come and talk to Mary's top half while I do things to her lower half." The combination was markedly successful – the spasm relaxed considerably and much good work was done at either end.' Psychotherapists may not be an essential feature of spas, but Dame Albertine Winner's characteristically vivid and pleasing pen picture epitomizes the quintessence of the holistic approach of spa therapy, integrating mind and body in its remedial regime.

Backing up this rapport between doctors and physiotherapists on the one hand, and patients on the other, is the social background of the spa, with advice, when necessary, on diet and exercise. Not all patients may be prepared to follow a strict regime of 'early to bed, early to rise', and a rigid diet, but they should be given the moral support to lead such a life if this is considered advisable on medical grounds. What the doctor must remember is that there is no such thing as 'doctor's orders'. Doctors do not order; they merely give advice. But the firmness with which this advice is given must vary according to the individual patient and his requirements. What is essential is that the patient must be able to relax, enjoy congenial company and good, though not necessarily exotic, food in a comfortable hotel amid pleasant surroundings in which he can indulge in the pleasures of life which appeal to him, whether this be golf, bird-watching, music, the theatre, or merely the joys of the countryside.

To list in their entirety the conditions which respond to spa therapy would be tedious. In short, however, they consist of: (1) All forms of rheumatism (though not in the acute phase) such as rheumatoid arthritis, osteoarthrosis, spondylitis, fibrositis, lumbago, sciatica, and gout. (2) Neurological, or nerve, disorders, such as poliomyelitis, those recovering from strokes, neuritis, nerve injuries, and some cases of Parkinsonism (or paralysis agitans as it is still sometimes known). (3) Patients who have had orthopaedic treatment for the results of accidents, such as fractures or injuries to joints. In addition, patients suffering from a poor circulation often benefit. These are all conditions for which the external use of the waters may be helpful. The conditions that may benefit from the drinking of the waters have already been discussed.

Such then is the rationale of spa therapy, a rationale which has satisfied mankind down the ages, and which it is the duty of the Department of Health and Social Security to restore to the citizens of this island home of ours, ensuring to them once again the services of spas that heal.

17

Spas and rheumatism

For all practical purposes, certainly in Great Britain, the two terms, spas and rheumatism, are synonymous at the present day. As indicated at the end of chapter 16, there are other conditions for which spa therapy is useful, but these constitute a minority of cases which could benefit from this traditional form of treatment. Yet, in spite of this close association between the two, today we are faced with the paradox that the upsurge in the public interest in rheumatism as a national problem is accompanied by the closure of the oldest of the great British spas. Like many human paradoxes it is a result of a combination of circumstances, including shortsightedness, professional self-interest and human stupidity. Some would say that this particular paradox is a classical example of the blind leading the blind.

Be all that as it may, the close interdependence of spas and rheumatism presents an intriguing problem worthy of careful consideration. The starting point may fairly be taken as the somewhat laboriously entitled document published by the British League Against Rheumatism and the Arthritis and Rheumatism Council to 'mark World Rheumatism Year 1977': *Rheumatism. The Price We Pay. The Impact of the Rheumatic Diseases on the Individual and the Country*. According to this, arthritis and rheumatism are 'the major cause of disruption and loss of work days in industry . . . consume more of the time of doctors than any other disease . . . and are twisting the lives and bodies of millions of people, both young and old.' 'Indeed', it concludes, 'the rheumatic diseases are so widespread that they are the biggest cause of pain and suffering this country, and indeed the world knows.' Further, 'Rheumatic disease is one of this country's – and the world's, major economic problems.'

The figures produced to substantiate these statements are quite impressive and are worth quoting in the convenient form they are presented in this pamphlet. Around 20 million people experience some form of rheumatic complaint during the course of a year, leading to the loss of 44 million days from work. This involves an annual loss in productivity of £420 million. There are at least half a million people with rheumatoid arthritis and 5 million with osteoarthrosis (or osteoarthritis as it used to be known: your modern scientific doctor loves to change the names of diseases). The total number with backache is not given, but a Government hand-out, reporting the setting up by the Department of Health and Social Security of a 'working group' (why not call it a committee?) to study the problem of back pain, states that it costs the nation 7 million working days lost and £100 million in sickness benefit and National Health Service treatment each year. To this may be added a comment of the Director of the Arthritis and Rheumatism Council Epidemiology Research Unit to the effect that, 'Back pain is rated third as a perceived threat to health by middle-aged people, coming after strokes and indigestion.' To him I am indebted for the following table showing the morbidity and the disability expressed as rates per thousand persons of both sexes for arthritis and rheumatism and for back pain:

	MORBIDITY	DISABILITY	
		All grades	*Severe*
Arthritis and rheumatism	79	21	7
Back and spine impairment	52	18	4

It is a gloomy picture that is painted, but, apparently, 'World Rheumatism Year [1977] will attempt to show not only the needs but also the achievements and the better forms of treatment and containment which exist for the sufferers if only sufficient medical facilities can be made available to pass them on.' But there is precious little said about treatment – and certainly nothing about spas, almost as if this term came into the category of those four-lettered words that should not be mentioned in polite company, or, in older terminology, as non-U. Something is said about research and much about organization, more specialists and the expenditure of more money on hospitals and the like.

In an attempt to brighten the picture it is claimed that, 'Treatment and surgery are alleviating crippling, suffering and pain.' 'And', it is added, 'if enough resources can be devoted to arthritis research and to getting the results to the patient through increased and better facilities the prospects are excellent for a cure for some of the most persistent forms of arthritis within the lifetime of most of the people reading this report.' This amazingly optimistic statement, more reminiscent of a Fleet Street headline than the publication of a professional organization, is capped by the equally incredible statement that, 'We have already conquered two rheumatic diseases which previously caused widespread suffering – rheumatic fever and gout.'

Neither of these diseases has been 'conquered' – unfortunately. Rheumatic fever has declined in incidence during the last forty years, but largely for unknown reasons. We are still ignorant of the fundamental cause and all that can be claimed is that by the prophylactic administration of penicillin its incidence can be reduced. Similarly with gout. It still exists, as all its victims know to their cost, and all that has happened is that drugs have been produced that can keep it under control in a certain proportion of cases. But it is still with us, and to claim that it has been 'conquered' is scientifically unjustified.

This atmosphere of optimism, amounting almost to euphoria, seems to be in the air at the moment, as exemplified by the recent claim of a senior member of the staff of the Royal National Hospital for Rheumatic Diseases in Bath that, 'The pace of, and investment into, research into rheumatoid arthritis is now so vast that it is difficult to conceive of anything less than victory in ten years, and the beginning of victory in five.' I am all for optimism, but I prefer it along the sober, justified lines indicated by Professor Duthie, whom I quote towards the end of this chapter.

I only hope the Bath physician is right, but I am not alone in failing to see the justification for his optimism. His statement reminded me of the claim made by my old friend, Sir Alexander Haddow, the experimental cancer expert, some ten years ago or more in introducing the current annual report of the British Empire Cancer Campaign, as it was known in those days, that in the sphere of cancer research, 'We had reached the beginning of the end.' It was a clever phrase that, as intended, appealed to the so-called 'medical correspondents' of Fleet Street and got the Report the additional publicity that was sought. The 'conquest' of cancer, however, is as far off as ever.

I am as keen as anyone for research into this baffling and important problem of rheumatism, and glad to know that between £2 and £3 million are spent every year on 'rheumatologically related research' by the Medical Research Council, the Department of Health and Social Security, and voluntary agencies like the Arthritis and Rheumatism Council. But I am somewhat worried about the way in which some of this research is developing. It is getting on for half a century since I first became involved in research into rheumatic diseases, and I am not particularly impressed with the progress that has been made. An unending series of theories have been produced but few have stood up to the test of time. The current one is that rheumatoid arthritis is what is known as an auto-immune disease. This is not the place to attempt to explain this theory which over the last few years has been advanced as the explanation of practically every disease for which no specific cause is known. Its protagonists ring the changes on it with the greatest of ease, and it must have been

The Hydrotherapy Department in use at the Royal National Hospital for Rheumatic Diseases, Bath. *Royal National Hospital for Rheumatic Diseases.*

responsible for more articles and M.D. and Ph.D. theses than any other invention of the mind of man.

The snag is that it has produced no practical contribution to the problem of how to prevent or treat the disease. The same applies to the other ever-recurring theory that rheumatoid arthritis is due to a virus. I must confess to having been one of the pioneers in advancing this theory. Some forty-odd years later I am interested to read in the annual report of the Medical Research Council Clinical Research Centre that a certain piece of research 'raises the question of a viral etiology of rheumatoid arthritis'.

The position so far as the other major rheumatic disease – osteoarthrosis – is concerned is just as pessimistic though not so complicated, and it is not unfair to say that we have really not advanced from the theory of my student days that this is a degenerative condition, partly of the ageing process, accelerated in some by other factors such as excessive or abnormal physical stresses or strains, as in sports and obesity.

The other criticism of modern rheumatic research is that it has become so diffuse that it has tended to get bogged down in what one might describe as the 'higher mathematics' of research. Even the most cursory glance at any of the rheumatic journals reveals how far away research has got from the practical problems, such as the value of spa therapy, facing those who are treating the disease. Indeed, one gets the impression that the research workers are much more interested in some of the auto-immune diseases, which can simulate rheumatoid arthritis for a time, such as the one known as systemic lupus erythematosus. What is tending to happen in Britain is what has already happened in the United States of America where, according to a recent report in the *British Medical Journal*, 'One-third of all papers of the recent American Rheumatism Association's scientific meeting at Miami Beach concerned systemic lupus erythematosus – hardly one of the more common problems of rheumatology. In contrast, only one clinical trial reported a treatment for rheumatoid arthritis and that was an uncontrolled anecdotal trial drawing unjustified conclusions from inadequate evidence.' 'If I had rheumatoid arthritis', the author adds, 'I would infinitely prefer to be treated over here.'

Equally, or even more, worrying are the dangers arising from modern drug treatment of rheumatic diseases. At one time this was restricted to aspirin, and there was no doubt of its pain-easing efficacy. There was a certain element of risk from its tendency to cause bleeding from the stomach in some patients if treatment in full doses was prolonged, as was often the case in rheumatoid arthritis. But in the old days, and still in the hands of careful physicians, this complication, or side-effect, to use a term that seems to slip as readily off the tongue of the layman as the doctor, was negligible compared with the benefits conferred in the relief of pain.

The pharmaceutical industry, however, decided to cash in on this potential market. A report on 'Prescribing in General Practice', published as a supplement to the *Journal of the Royal College of General Practitioners* in 1972, showed that analgesics (pain-relieving) drugs were the most frequently advertised to doctors, followed closely by drugs for the treatment of rheumatic diseases and gout. Simultaneously a stream of anti-rheumatic drugs gushed forth from the factory, not one of which is a real improvement on aspirin. Some may be as good (though much more expensive), but all have side-effects. In the words of a former research director of one of our largest pharmaceutical companies, 'all of them cause trouble in the alimentary canal, sometimes ulceration.'

This was dramatized in characteristically Hibernian style by a leading Dublin physician who was quoted by *The Times* as saying that, 'The Duke of Edinburgh would be better off taking a few aspirins before playing polo rather than the drug Butazolidin with which he has admitted having dosed himself to stay in the game.' *The Times* report continued: '"If you have got to the age when exercise hurts, have physiotherapy and get fit before your game of golf or polo," he said. Taking drugs is likely to do more harm than good in the long run. It was "not desirable" that people should dose themselves with drugs like Butazolidin, which was normally given only under close medical supervision. It could produce serious side-effects in some cases. "I have had seven patients who died from the use of it."'

Even more alarming is the use of much more dangerous drugs such as penicillamine, for instance, of which it has been said that 'Seven fatalities attributable to the drug have been reported, and more cases will undoubtedly arise,' and a report from Toronto describes the development of fatal acute leukaemia in two patients with rheumatoid arthritis treated with another of the potent drugs now being used in the treatment of the disease. Lest I be thought to be prejudiced, biased or unfair in this sphere, let me quote from two reviews of a recently published textbook on rheumatology,

According to one, referring to the leukaemia-inducing drug, 'Fears that long-term treatment could produce malignancy have not yet been substantiated.' According to the other, discussing drug treatment, 'We still do not know what are the best treatments for these diseases.'

The extent to which drugs are being used in the treatment of rheumatic diseases is evident from the fact that in England alone more than £20 million is being spent annually on prescription costs for rheumatic diseases, and this, it has been noted, is 'an underestimate because only certain classes of drugs can be identified'.

Not so disturbing, but indicating a lack of balance in the approach to the problem, is the increasing extent to which the surgeons are being called in to patch up rheumatic patients. As one rheumatologist has proudly put it: 'Productive close relations have developed with surgical rheumatologists, who are now replacing so many damaged joints that they have created a crisis of supply.' And what for all I know may be a typical example of this surgical enthusiasm is reported from Glasgow: 'Mr M., now 51, off work, and for most of the time housebound, has suffered from rheumatoid arthritis for the last twenty-four years. He has a MacIntosh prosthesis in each knee, a pinned hip, a couple of silastic joints in his right hand and has had seven synovectomies [removal of the lining of a joint] to his hand and elbows.'

Surely this is the antithesis of the traditional healing art. Yet it is encouraged by the Arthritis and Rheumatism Council, which has incorporated a department of orthopaedic surgery in the new Bone and Joint Research Unit which it has just established at The London Hospital at a cost of £500,000. By all means encourage research into the rheumatic diseases but let it be devoted to the prevention of the diseases and a study of the rationale of old-established methods of treatment such as spa therapy, which may not cure (neither does surgery) but does at least bring relief to the patient without all the trauma and risk of an operation.

That the public is not satisfied with the care and treatment they are receiving from their orthodox doctors (or allopaths as they used to be known to differentiate them from homoeopaths and unorthodox practitioners such as osteopaths) is clear from the fact that an estimated 277,000 handicapped or impaired persons have consulted an oestopath or a chiropractor at some time, the great majority of whom are likely to have been suffering from a rheumatic disease. According to the survey upon which these figures are based, of those who sought the heterodox advice of osteopaths and chiropractors, two-thirds of the very severely handicapped said they had been helped, whereas this was true of only one-third of the impaired.

The conclusion reached is that around 200,000 people consult an osteopath or a chiropractor during the course of a year, a figure similar to those for new attendances at rheumatology and rehabilitation outpatient clinics. As has been noted by the Arthritis and Rheumatism Council, 'The existence of 430 qualified osteopaths and chiropractors and approximately 3000 unqualified persons able to earn their livelihood by offering alternative treatments for rheumatic disorders has complex causes. Nevertheless, as an indication of public confidence in the accomplishments of general practitioners it can hardly be regarded as encouraging.'

A more reasoned review of the problem is that of the Director of the Council's Epidemiology Unit:

> 'The nub of the problem, of course, is the doubts that exist about the effectiveness of heterodox treatment. Samuel Pepys epitomized the fundamental uncertainty in his diary: "I am at a loss to know whether it be my hare's foot which is my preservative, or my taking of a pill of turpentine every morning" . . . The allopath is often similarly at a loss about his own activities, wondering whether the patient got better in spite or because of them. The problem is further compounded by the perennial dilemma of rheumatology and rehabilitation, uncertainty whether what we observe is attributable to the therapy or to the therapist . . .

> 'Both allopaths and the heterodox practitioners need to recognize that what matters is whether a procedure is effective; why it may be so is immaterial until one is assured that it is effective . . . Moreover, the theoretical foundation for much orthodox practice is either frankly pragmatic or as dubious as that of heterodox practice: to withdraw into a shell of theoretical plausibility or purity is vain protection . . . Successful practice doesn't necessarily mean one has altered the natural history of the patient's condition. It may signify only that one has been kind or sympathetic, or that something concrete has been done and that you have projected your own confidence.'

This surely is the philosophy of spa therapy, and the practical application is to be seen in an account of the treatment of rheumatoid arthritis as practised by Professor J. J. R. Duthie and his colleagues of the department of rheumatology in the Edinburgh Medical School. Basically this consists, for the acute case, of rest in bed with the application of plaster splints to the affected joints to ensure that they are kept at complete rest. Aspirin is given 'to the limits of tolerance', and appropriate methods of physiotherapy are used. As the acute phase of the disease passes there is a gradual reduction in the dosage of aspirin and a gradual increase in the amount of exercise until the 'highest functional level' of the patient's muscles and joints is achieved. Drugs other than aspirin are avoided. The report, which includes a nine-year follow-up of over 300 patients, some of whom had been followed for the full nine years, notes that, 'Treatment in addition to the basic regime appeared to convey no additional benefit.'

But perhaps the most significant feature of this report is what it has to say about the management of the patient as opposed to the disease. This starts off with the comment that, 'A study of social and economic factors indicated a close relationship between domestic or financial difficulties and the degree of crippling, as might be expected, but the relatively small number of unresolved problems at the last assessment was a clear indication of the important part played by medical social workers in the long-term care of the disabled. Maintenance or loss of morale was also intimately related to the degree of disability.' 'The training of these patients', the report continues, 'while in hospital in the use of splints, home physiotherapy, and remedial exercises in conjunction with subsequent regular medical supervision may largely account for their more favourable course.' 'If these conclusions are valid', the report ends, 'they certainly constitute a powerful argument in favour of hospital treatment early in the disease and for the provision of adequate medical and social supervision after discharge.'

This is a point that Professor Duthie repeatedly emphasizes, as is exemplified in the following excerpt from the chapter on 'Chronic Rheumatic Diseases' which he contributes to probably the best-known textbook of treatment in the English language. 'It cannot be too strongly emphasized that treatment embraces the management of the patient as well as measures which aim at relieving the disease. The first consideration in the treatment of chronic rheumatic disease is to secure the co-operation of the patient. It should be explained that dramatic results must not be expected and that reliance should be placed on the judicious application not of one form of treatment but of a combination of methods which have been carefully thought out. His confidence won, his co-operation secured and the fundamental principles underlying correct treatment observed, a prospect of progressive improvement lies before the patient. Treated early and adequately, the outlook in the severe forms of chronic rheumatic disease is far from being as gloomy as has been formerly held by the laity and the profession.'

Than which there could be no better introduction to the final chapter on 'Spas Today and Tomorrow'.

18

Spas today and tomorrow

In the past, as we have seen, spas have subserved a most useful function. Our primitive forebears, not to mention the animal kingdom in general, soon recognized the healing power of water and took full advantage of it. This healing power may have been partly mystical, superstitious, religious, call it what you will, but what of it? What is this but in modern scientific jargon, psychosomatic medicine – the recognition that mind and body are one and interdependent? This knowledge of, and belief in, the healing power of water was taken over by succeeding civilizations, and for long, certainly during the great Greek, Roman and Alexandrian civilizations, was one of the great standbys of medical practice. Indeed, it could legitimately be described as the major form of therapy.

Following the fall of the Roman Empire it fell into disuse in Europe, though not in Mohammedan countries, to be revived around the time of the Renaissance, and from then on it assumed an ever-increasing importance in the treatment of disease. To a certain extent this may have been partly due to the lack of potent drugs. Certainly, after the introduction of anaesthesia and of antiseptics, which made surgery safe, followed by the drug explosion initiated in the latter part of the nineteenth century, the indications for spa therapy were considerably curtailed.

In time this meant that its main value was in the treatment of the rheumatic diseases or any other condition, such as poliomyelitis or strokes, which resulted in any form of crippling. For these, spa waters were used externally in the form of baths. Internally they were taken for indigestion and kidney disorders. Over the years the treatment became more scientific and more varied. While still essentially based on the use of water, or hydrotherapy, this was combined with exercises and massage. In addition, various forms of electrotherapy were introduced though, to a certain extent, these are now tending to be discarded.

Today the position is that spas are flourishing in the majority of continental countries. This is attributed by their critics to fashion and high-powered salesmanship on the part of their owners – whether private, State or civic. Undoubtedly this factor does come into play, as judged by some of the more exuberant brochures in glorious technicolour issued by continental spas. But this is a minor consideration, and what must weigh with any impartial observer is the fact that spa therapy is recognized – and paid for – by the equivalent of our National Health Service on both sides of the Iron Curtain.

It is difficult to believe that the powers that be in France and Germany, for instance, would spend the large sums of money they do every year in sending patients to spas unless they felt that this was economically and medically justified. Equally, it is difficult to believe that the doctors of these countries would continue to recommend spa therapy unless they considered that it was a legitimate and beneficial form of treatment. Granted that there may be an element of vested interest here on the part of doctors in spas, but this cannot explain the wellnigh universal use of spas by the vast majority of doctors.

Incidentally, current developments in spa therapy in Western (non-Communist) Europe represent an interesting version of the social revolution that is gradually engulfing the capitalist world. At one time, patronized by the aristocracy, the 'gentry' and the well-to-do classes, with recognized seasons when 'Society' foregathered in luxurious surroundings to take the waters and follow a regime based on iron, but unwritten, laws laid down by long-established social etiquette and precedence, spas are now becoming 'democratized' and the haunts of all sections of the community. So much so that, for example, at formerly fashionable spas such as Vichy, hotels with international reputations are having to close down or lower their standards because visitors are not prepared, or able, to pay their charges. In some places these old-time 'palaces' are being converted into hostels where large numbers of trade unionists can be accommodated in reasonable, but modest, comfort at charges they can meet.

Before finally leaving this point about the continued support of spa therapy by continental governments and doctors, it is of interest to note that, as mentioned in chapter 15, the Danish Government is prepared to lay out relatively large sums to send patients with psoriasis for treatment at an Israeli spa on the shores of the Dead Sea. This they are doing on the recommendation of Danish doctors. Here, apart from anything else, is a case where there is no vested interest on the part of either government or doctors.

One of the criticisms advanced of spa therapy is that it is not scientific, that it is all in the mind and that the patient simply feels better because of the psychological effect of the pleasant surroundings, the distractions provided by the spa, whether these be physical, mental, emotional or aesthetic, and the close personal attention he receives from those in attendance on him, particularly physiotherapists. The brief answer to this is that if the patient feels better, has less pain and less stiffness and is able to return home looser in limb and freer in action, then something worthwhile has been achieved. And, as I hope has been made clear in this book, a well-organized spa can achieve this better than a hospital hydrotherapy department. (Hospitals, it has been said, are places to be avoided unless you are really ill and require treatment that cannot be effectively given elsewhere, and the shorter the stay in hospital the better.)

A period of treatment in hospital is needed for an acute exacerbation of rheumatoid arthritis, but for the treatment of the chronic phase – to keep it under control, if not to cure it – the equivalent of outpatient treatment is indicated. Whilst much of this can be effectively given in a hospital hydrotherapy department for those not living in or near a spa, this is not the same as treatment in a modern spa. As has been indicated, the ideal is regular courses of spa therapy, interleaved, if necessary, with treatment as a hospital outpatient, though in quite a number of cases treatment can be maintained at home, the patient continuing with the exercises he has been taught at the spa, whether in his bedroom or his bath, taking his prescribed baths and applying heat when needed from such excellent sources as a gas fire.

It is this over-all, continuing treatment that is so valuable and produces such beneficial effects, and the nub of it all is regular spa therapy. I am not suggesting for one moment that hospital hydrotherapy is useless. Applied properly, and with the requisite moral support automatically provided by the well-trained physiotherapist, it is an excellent second best, but it has not the over-all beneficial effect of spa therapy.

This non-specific effect of spa treatment, so strongly criticized by certain rheumatologists (some of whom ought to know better) is part and parcel of what the laity has come to know as the placebo response. In brief, this means the improvement the patient feels no matter what treatment he is given, provided he has sufficient faith in it. Much denounced by the modern scientific doctor, it is a perfectly legitimate form of treatment. In this context it is of interest to note what one of our most experienced London rheumatologists has to say on the subject.

'The ancient and modern spas . . . still have their appeal, as they had to the ancient Romans and the Ephesians before them . . . Warmth, rest, relaxation, and the proper diet for the individual concerned are all good treatment . . . There is no harm in inducing a placebo response . . . Indeed, through the ages, this is essentially what, with analgesics [pain-relieving drugs], rest, and simple measures the rheumatoid sufferer has been getting in the past, and what in some cases he is still getting today.' In this last sentence some would change 'some cases' to 'most cases'.

If this sitting-on-the-fence attitude is not a full justification of modern spa therapy, then, in the words of an older generation, 'I'm a Dutchman'. Particularly is this the case when one takes into consideration a further statement in the article from which I have just quoted: 'Natural remission occurs fairly often in rheumatoid arthritis and this explains why long-continued treatment of any variety may sometimes appear to produce remission. Drugs that do reverse the inflammatory reaction in rheumatoid arthritis, such as the corticosteroids, are rapidly followed by relapse on stopping the drug. In general, whatever happens to be the drug of the moment tends to get the credit for what is often, in fact, an inexplicable natural remission.'

In other words, your modern rheumatologist, no matter how scientific his approach, or how isolated he may be in his ivory tower, has little, if anything, to add to what patients receive at spas. He may talk glibly about his specialty having 'developed its own diagnostic and treatment skills such as arthroscopy, synoviography and intra-articular injection', as another modern rheumatologist has done, but all too often these are merely meddlesome interference. As research tools, used by experts under controlled conditions, they are undoubtedly of value, but as routine measures they must be regarded with considerable suspicion.

Again, let me hasten to say that I have no objection to research. Rather am I all for it. I should hate to tot up the number of children whom I have used as 'human guinea-pigs', and I hasten to add that they – and their parents – all remained good friends of mine. To these adorable children convalescing from acute rheumatism, and all too many of them already showing ominous signs of incipient heart disease, in whom I caused any transitory discomfort I offer my long-delayed apologies. Later I became interested in a new technique known as plasmapharesis, and the last grant I received from the Medical Research Council was to allow me to use this method for the investigation of the proteins in joint fluids in healthy and rheumatic subjects.

What worries me today – and I am not alone in this – is that clinical research has become the equivalent of the Biblical golden calf, and that in prostrating themselves at its feet all too many doctors are forgetting that the prime consideration of clinical research is the betterment of patients. Increase in human knowledge is merely incidental.

Which brings me to the only reasonable criticism of spa therapy. This, as we have seen, is that there is no advantage in spa waters as compared with ordinary water, and therefore that a well-run hospital hydrotherapy department can provide as effective treatment as a spa. Ignoring for the moment all the ancillary advantages of a spa compared with a hospital department, the answer to this criticism is that there is evidence that spa waters, with their varying constituents, do have an effect on the body different from that of ordinary water. Granted – and I am the first to admit it – this is a point that has not been investigated carefully enough, and continental investigators have made all too many statements for which they have not the evidence. On the other hand, it is a much more difficult problem than it would appear to be superficially. Particularly is this so if the high standards of modern medical statistics are to be maintained.

While this does not excuse the protagonists of spa therapy from tending to take the line of least resistance, ignoring the fundamental scientific problem, and resting their claims predominantly on the results they can show, neither does it justify the anti-spa school in their current attitude. If they wish to damn and abolish spas, then let them produce scientific evidence, based on carefully controlled trials, indicating that spa waters have no advantages over tap water. Until they do this, they have no more justification in condemning spa therapy than the spa advocates have in proclaiming their merits. And the latter have the great advantage that they can produce so many patients – all down the ages – who have benefited from the spas that heal.

'Benefited', it will be noted; not 'cured'. This is an important difference, and one which the anti-spa school make much of. They refer to the 'cures' claimed by spas, and the traditional reference to patients 'taking the cure' at spas. I am as fussy as anyone about the use and misuse of the word 'cure', and my pernicketiness on this point has more than once embroiled me in arguments with my colleagues and my readers. But I was brought up professionally by a chief who would not allow the word to be used in his ward register. Patients, he always contended, recovered; they were not cured. A humbling thought which I have always appreciated having had drilled into me in my early professional days.

Where the spa critics are wrong here, is that in spa circles the word 'cure' comes from the German *Kur*, which means treatment or course of treatment. Thus all that was meant by 'taking the cure' was to be under treatment, or, in German, *in der Kur sein*. So much for this unjustified playing with words in an attempt to destroy the reputation of spas as valuable resorts of the healing art.

It is against this background that the problem must be considered of why at the present moment there is only one functioning spa left in the United Kingdom. The simple answer is that the medical profession – or at least that section of it concerned with rheumatology – advised the Minister of Health, or his successor the Secretary of State (whom, for the sake of simplicity, I shall henceforth refer to as the Minister) that they subserved no useful function and could therefore be closed. Too often the blame is laid upon the Minister. This is not so. In my time I have been as critical as anyone of the National Health Service, though I still consider that it is the best service of its kind in the world but, so far as spas are concerned, the Minister is free from criticism. The simple reason for this is that, possibly with one notable (some would say notorious) female exception, successive Ministers have lent over backwards in avoiding any semblance of interfering with the clinical judgments of doctors. Some would say that they have leant over too far in this respect, and I must confess there have been occasions when, even as an old-fashioned (Asquithian) liberal (without a capital), I have wondered whether this might be the case. On the whole, however, it was erring on the right side, and what is clear is that no Minister would have closed down, or approved the closing down, of a spa treatment centre if this had not been recommended on the part of the medical profession.

Why rheumatologists took up this attitude was a combination of circumstances, which need not be discussed in detail here though it is quite a fascinating study in the vagaries of human nature. (Doctors, in spite of what some of the more abrasive members of the Patients' Association say, are only human.) Three main factors, however, were involved.

The first, though not necessarily the most important, was that the post-1945 generation of rheumatologists developed an inferiority complex. They felt that they were not being given the specialist status to which they were entitled, and that they were being loaded with a rag-bag of cases with which their specialist colleagues could not cope – what, with characteristic candour, Lord Horder once described as 'the flotsam and jetsam of his medical and surgical colleagues'. Many physicians treated their own cases of rheumatoid arthritis, and the only patients referred to the rheumatologists were those requiring some form of physiotherapy. The result was that, while undoubtedly there were able doctors among the ranks of rheumatologists, particularly in the case of the London teaching hospitals and some of the spas, notably Bath, Buxton and Harrogate, the specialty such as it was, tended to collect more than its fair share of the 'also-rans' or 'failed specialists' of the profession.

This was a state of affairs that did not appeal to the younger generation of potential specialists on returning to civilian life after the Second World War. Particularly was this the case with those who had been privileged to participate in the superb rehabilitation service that the Armed Forces had developed to ensure that the wounded and the sick were returned to active service as quickly as possible. It was these bright young men who wanted to continue this work in the wider sphere of rheumatology and who insisted on rheumatology being purged of all the hangers-on and camp followers it had accumulated over the years.

Once having had their claims as specialists admitted by the Royal College of Physicians of London, they then started an internecine war on what their specialty included. The main bugbear here was the fact that hitherto departments of what they now wanted to be known as 'rheumatology' had been known as 'departments of physical medicine'. Incidentally, this latter title really only went back some twenty years: it was in 1921 that The London Hospital was a pioneer in appointing a physician-in-charge of physical medicine. The difference in opinion is admirably shown by two quotations, one from a member of the older generation in 1952, the other from one of the younger generation (actually one of my old students) in 1970.

According to the former: 'It seemed a pity that certain specialists in Physical Medicine should have shown a desire to fragment the subject by the erection of a separate "specialty" of Rheumatology.' According to the latter: 'The march of events has dictated a change of name . . . We can no longer tolerate a name [Physical Medicine] which gives such an erroneous impression of our true functions in medicine.' A further complication was that the Royal College of Physicians had recommended that this new specialty should include rehabilitation. Whilst this concept was accepted by some, others scorned it, as represented by the following quotation: 'Rheumatology is now a well-defined specialty within the field of general medicine requiring a high degree of skill and experience, leaving no time for undertaking additional responsibilities in the more general field of medical rehabilitation.'

The main factor, however, was the belief of the rising generation of rheumatologists that their specialty must become more scientific. The art of medicine as practised since the days of Hippocrates must be subjugated to the rule of science, and no practice should be approved unless it could be supported by science. It was therefore essential that all unscientific appurtenances such as spas should be eradicated and the specialty should only be practised in the scientifically controlled precincts of a hospital, whether this practice included hydrotherapy, electrotherapy, massage, exercises, or a combination of the lot. Hence their recommendation that spas were dispensable.

In these circumstances it is not surprising that successive Ministers seized the opportunity to cut the cost of their subvention to spas. Particularly so as it was a plausible argument that was advanced. Unfortunately, it was a basically unsound one. Science is the handmaiden, not the mistress, of medicine, and the art of medicine must never be subservient to science. Only when there is definitive proof of its value can science be incorporated in the practice of medicine, and as often as not, the contributions of science are ancillary to the healing art. One of the wise old adages that the younger generation has forgotten is that the older generation knew a great deal about their patients, but less about the science of treatment, while the younger generation know a great deal about the science of treatment but less about the patient as an individual.

This is why, until convincing evidence to the contrary is produced, spas must continue to be an integral part of the healing art. It is in co-operation with spas that our departments of rheumatology can make their greatest contribution – and undoubtedly they have a valuable contribution to make – to the solving of this age-old problem of the rheumatic diseases that disable and cripple so many of our fellow-citizens today. And, if the nation is to obtain full value from the money spent on these departments, the spotlight of research must be switched on to our spas, and much more money spent on probing into their *modus operandi* than on producing, for example, an endless stream of dangerous drugs.

So what of tomorrow? The position today, as we have seen, is that there is only one functioning spa in the United Kingdom, and it is functioning to everyone's satisfaction. There are another seven which are viable though non-functioning at the moment:

Bath, Buxton, Droitwich, Harrogate, Llandrindod Wells, Strathpeffer, and Woodhall Spa. All of these have been visited in the course of writing this book.

The last of these to close was Bath – in December 1976. Until then it had been treating predominantly National Health Service patients, the responsible authority being the Bath City Council, which received an annual allocation from the National Health Service based upon the number of patients treated. This still left a balance to be paid out of the rates. It was because the Department of Health and Social Security stopped this subsidy, and the Bath City Council refused to make any further contribution to the cost of the Spa Treatment Centre that the latter was closed.

As explained in chapter 5, there was no justification for this step. The major cause was lack of foresight on the part of the City Fathers, and lack of support from the local consultants. To remedy the situation an appeal has been opened for £250,000 to resurrect the spa as an active treatment centre. To this extent, at the moment, the brightest prospect for reactivation is Bath.

The closure of Droitwich in 1976 was even more reprehensible than that of Bath in that the brine baths of Droitwich are unique in Britain if not in Europe, and even the scientifically biased doctors have to admit that there is sound evidence in favour of their efficacy.

The development of Buxton as a spa has been taken up by the British Tourist Authority, but at the moment no-one seems to be interested in Harrogate, Llandrindod Wells, Strathpeffer or Woodhall Spa. Nevertheless, all four of these are viable.

In the following centres there are National Health Service hospitals where the local rheumatologists, who would also have medical control of the Spa Treatment Centres, would be able to treat those patients who needed inpatient treatment, and the ancillary staff, predominantly physiotherapists, would be shared between the hospital and the Spa Treatment Centre.

If these seven spas could be brought back into action the country would have a series of valuable treatment centres for rheumatic and other crippling conditions scattered strategically throughout the length and breadth of the land:

Strathpeffer to cover Scotland
Llandrindod Wells to cover Wales
Buxton to cover North-West England
Harrogate to cover North-East England and Yorkshire
Leamington and Droitwich to cover the West Midlands
Woodhall Spa to cover East Anglia and the East Midlands
Bath to cover South-West and South-East England

The two outstanding problems are cost and accommodation. So far as the latter is concerned, this would involve providing sufficient hotels and hostels to allow patients to stay in the spa for periods ranging as a rule from two to four weeks. At the present cost of living, hotels of the requisite standard are expensive, but there is no reason why the larger hotel organizations which we now have should not be able to help here – to their financial benefit. After all if, as is the case in London, one of the largest hotel groups has found it worthwhile to invest in a private hospital, there is no reason why they and their opposite numbers should not exploit the possibilities in such attractive centres as Bath, Buxton, Harrogate, Llandrindod Wells and Woodhall Spa. To encourage them to do so there might well be Government help in the way of allowances in the form of subsidies such as have already been granted to the hotel industry, and also local authority help in the form of rating relief and the like. The more a spa flourishes the more beneficial is it to the ratepayers.

But no matter how enterprising hoteliers may be, there will still be a need for cheaper accommodation in the form of what might be described as hostels or, if you like, convalescent homes. Here an obvious contribution could be made by the larger trade unions, following the example of their opposite numbers on the other side of the Iron Curtain. A number of trade unions already run convalescent homes for their members. Has the time not come when they could usefully provide hostels for their rheumatic members and their members recovering from accidents in the seven spas I have listed? This would be of particular value to those trade unions with more vulnerable members, such as the National Union of Mineworkers, the Transport and General Workers Union, the National Union of Seamen, and the National Union of Railwaymen. It would not require a very big levy on each member to provide hostels for this purpose, especially as the return in the improved health and wage-earning capacity of those afflicted members would be considerably increased.

In addition, Government – and local-authority – sponsored hostels might well be organized and run without too great, if any, financial loss. In practically all the centres mentioned there must be large houses, or groups of houses, that could be taken over for this purpose, thus avoiding the current high costs of building.

The cost of running the Spa Treatment Centres would not be high when looked at with comparable costs in the National Health Service. Neither should the cost of reopening them be high. Bath has already committed itself to an appeal to retrieve the situation as quickly as possible. As this appeal was launched in World Rheumatism Year, is it asking too much for the organizers of the latter to make a large contribution to this appeal a first call on their funds? Indeed, the revival of British spas should be a major interest here. There is a tendency for the collector of funds for rheumatism to get research out of perspective. For instance, would it not have been more to the point for the Arthritis and Rheumatism Council to have contributed the whole of the £250,000 necessary for the reopening of the Bath Spa Treatment Centre, rather than spend £500,000 on the building and fitting up of the new Bone and Joint Research Unit opened early in 1977 in the London Hospital Medical School? Much of the work being done in this Unit was already being done equally effectively elsewhere in the London Hospital. Half the money spent in reviving Bath as a spa, and half on research devoted to investigating the true value of the Bath thermal waters would have produced much

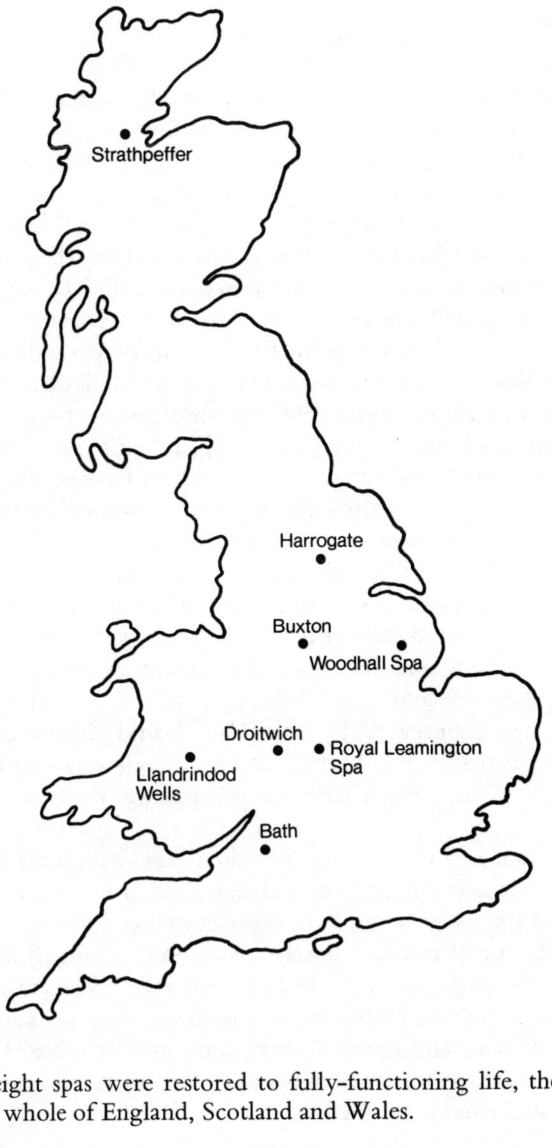

If these eight spas were restored to fully-functioning life, they could serve the whole of England, Scotland and Wales.

better dividends. One of these days those responsible for planning and subsidizing research will relearn the old lesson that money spent on bricks and mortar is money largely wasted.

From the cost angle, attention would also need to be devoted to private, or paying, patients – as on the continent. There must be quite a number of middle-aged or elderly well-to-do patients who would be grateful for the opportunity of receiving the benefits of spa therapy in this country rather than having to travel abroad. In any case why, as we are doing at the moment, make it necessary to take currency out of the country to get spa treatment when we are perfectly capable of providing equally good facilities at home? It is here that the British Tourist Authority should adopt a more aggressive and enterprising policy in build-up our spas as holiday centres, not only for our own citizens, but also for visitors from overseas. What spa in Europe, for instance, can offer anything comparable to Stratford-upon-Avon, Kenilworth, Warwick, Malvern and the Three Choirs' Festival – all within easy reach of Droitwich and Leamington?

And if even more cash is required, what about casinos – one of the main financial sources for many a continental spa? I hold no brief for casinos and have seldom known anything more depressing than the only one I have ever visited, but they are now legal in this country. Why therefore should the local or civic authority concerned not open casinos in all seven spas I have listed and devote the profits to subsidizing the spa treatment centres?

Such then are the spas of Britain today and tomorrow. Inevitably this is no more than a sketchy outline of what could be done. On the other hand, I am quite convinced that it is no pipe-dream. As Sir Winston Churchill once said at our 'finest hour': 'Give us the tools, and we will finish the job.' Here are eight spas with a long and honourable history in the healing art. Let us adopt them forthwith and convert them into spas that heal for many years to come, to the greater benefit of an increasing number of crippled and rheumatic citizens.

Index

Note: Numbers in italic refer to illustrations